PRACTICAL SURVIVAL
SKILLS

NATURE'S LARDER: WILD FOODS SURVIVAL GUIDE

J.P. LOGAN

INTRODUCTION

If you are the kind of person who is drawn to nature and enjoys spending a lot of time outdoors, you may have often wondered about whether or not you could actually survive out there using nothing more than your own skills and instincts to get by. Chances are, probably not. Modern humans as a whole have become rather fragile, and we are far too reliant upon the conveniences and technological advancements that make our lives too easy. From running water, to electricity, grocery stores and the Internet, we have lost touch with the self-reliant abilities that helped our ancestors to survive and thrive in the natural world.

However, there is no need to be dismayed. With a little bit of dedication, perseverance, and insight, surviving in the wilderness is still entirely possible and within our reach. Nature can provide all that we need in life. There are thousands of plants to nibble on; creatures to hunt down and eat; ingenious methods for finding, purifying, and storing safe drinking water; and different ways to exploit the environment for constructing shelters, weapons, and tools. If you are driven by a curiosity and passion for the natural world, knowing how to survive in an unexpected situation is essential.

Survivalism is not only for conspiracy theorists who hoard walls and walls of canned goods in their underground bunkers. Survivalism is something that every child should be taught from a young age and a skill that should be practiced and honed throughout our lives into adulthood. Whether you are a family man or a solo traveler; someone with great aspirations for adventure or a person who enjoys watching the sunset; or whether you simply want to be prepared for disasters, worst-case scenarios, and crises in the wilderness, survivalism can serve you and enrich your life to the fullest. It is also important for people that love adventure sports, off-grid living, and for homesteaders to learn how to survive in various conditions. It can help keep you and your loved ones alive in precarious situations, and it also serves as an important way to reconnect with nature and all that our ancestors worked and fought for. With the current state of the world—global supply chain volatility; food shortages in stores and supermarkets; unanticipated effects of pandemics and subsequent lockdowns; and the ominous effects of climate change on the reliability and yields of our crops —we should all be making efforts to prepare for, and expect, the unexpected. These skills are essential for an ever-changing world that not only we are living in but our children as well.

Allow this book to be your guide. In it, you will learn how to find nourishment from your environment without poisoning yourself or dying from starvation. You will be able to learn how to cook, disinfect, and purify various foods to ensure they are safe and ready for consumption. Nobody wants to die reeling in pain from stomach issues, dysentery, or slowly sucked dry by internal parasites.

But first, let me tell you a little bit more about myself. I am a husband, father, and retired member of the military. I have always loved the great outdoors—reveling in its grandeur. Whether that means going out on a fishing trip by myself; camping with my wife and children; or taking a difficult hike with my friends, connecting with the natural world is very important to me.

During my time in the army, my appreciation for the wild helped me to survive many perilous situations where others may not have fully prevailed. I am trained in wild foraging, wildcrafting, and bushcraft. I am a certified wilderness first-aid responder, and I deeply care about people who find themselves in distressing situations while trying to enjoy the great outdoors. It is my strong belief that we need to return to their wild, ancestral capabilities. I want to help more people prepare for the unexpected so that they, too, will be able to survive.

I founded the "Wilderness Survival Community Center" to do just that. Now, I have the great joy and pleasure of sharing my skills and knowledge with others, teaching them how to survive when outdoors, leading seminars on wild edibles, cooking outdoors, and sustaining yourself on the bare essentials. It is one of my greatest desires that more people are able to live off of the land, using their own skills, innovation, and knowledge of nature and all that it has to offer to us. This is my second book on survivalism, complementing my previous work, *Practical Survival Skills: First Aid & Natural Medicines You Need to Know to Keep You Healthy & Fit In a Survival Situation.*

DIVING INTO SOME PRACTICAL SURVIVAL SKILLS

This is a survival food guide for when you find yourself trapped in the wild. Use it wisely, but understand that no single book will be able to tell you all that there is to know about survivalism, the wild, or foraging. You need to take charge of your own learning journey, seek out more information, and build up a library of survival knowledge to use now and in the future.

This book will provide some comprehensive information on how to find, prepare, cook, and eat many different kinds of plants, roots, bugs, insects, and other animals that are found in nature's vast larder.

There are step-by-step instructions on how to provide for yourself and the others around you as well as how to find nourishment so that you can escape your perilous situation. You will learn about wild berries, poisonous plants, edible roots, and how to make foods safe to eat and enjoy. You can gain confidence in your abilities to discern between safe and unsafe options, and you will learn how to successfully survive any outdoor mishap, sudden disaster, or unexpected survival situation that may come your way.

This book will cover some of nature's most delectable, abundant, as well as less desirable yet sustaining foods, including greens, berries, fruits, roots, tubers, insects, more creepy crawlies, small game, and large game. There will be a comprehensive "Wild Edibles Index" in Chapter 7 that will go over multiple categories and further explain more information on these survival foods.

We will look into exactly how to go about foraging for natural edibles including where you can find them and how to discern between different varieties. You will also need to know how to prepare and cook wild edibles—something that should always be done for safety reasons. You can cook without the need for electricity in many different ways—most of which require a fire. Building a fire requires several steps including the collection of materials, setting up a safe fire pit, and actually igniting your materials. These are all necessary steps for ensuring you can disinfect not only food but also water so that you don't get sick.

No prior skills or knowledge will be necessary for you to reap the benefits of this book. You can easily learn exactly what to look out for in different kinds of environments and situations. These skills and knowledge will help you feel confident, self-reliant, and independent in the wilderness. With this book as your guide, you will be ready to face whatever surprises may come your way on your journey.

FORAGING 101

FEAR OF FORAGING

In today's modern world, with all our creature comforts and safety nets, foraging can seem not only intimidating but downright dangerous. When the topic of foraging comes up in my survival seminars, I often hear expressions of fear and trepidation: "I'm too scared to go foraging because I don't feel confident in identifying anything," or "I don't want to poison myself like that guy in the movie!" It can be easy to forget that our ancestors not only lived but thrived in natural habitats without access to electricity or running water —all by simply relying on the land. Of course, we cannot overlook the fact that they had developed their knowledge over thousands of years and hundreds of generations, constantly working to improve, improvise, and overcome any challenge that came their way. It is also quite scary to think about being thrust into an unknown habitat, with no tools or resources, and having to fend entirely for yourself. However, like any skill, foraging is something that is developed and honed over time. You do not need to know everything, and we must all begin somewhere. Nobody starts as an expert —including myself. The most important factors are an appreciation for the natural world and a desire to learn.

"The more that you read, the more things you will know. The more that you learn, the more places you'll go."

— DR. SEUSS

BASIC RULES OF FORAGING

So what exactly is "foraging"? Foraging is simply the means of acquiring food from nature—it can include hunting animals; fishing; gathering plants and fungi; and scavenging on the efforts of other animals when the opportunity presents itself to you. Survivalists, herbalists, and nature enthusiasts can all agree on a few simple rules and guidelines that will help to keep not only yourself safe but also the environment in which you find yourself while out foraging. As foragers, it is our responsibility to use nature's resources wisely and respectfully.

1. **Be aware of your surroundings:** It is crucial to understand the type of environment and landscapes in which you may find yourself. How likely are you to run into a bear or dangerous animal? Is there access to freshwater? Are there venomous spiders to consider while outdoors? What is the chance of falling off a high cliff or into a raging river? How hot or cold does it get? Are there things to look out for like deep crevices, sinkholes, or caves?

2. **Never go alone:** If you do, always make sure that someone knows where you are and inform them of the intended length of your excursions.

3. **Wear personal protective equipment:** Use gloves when harvesting prickly or spiny plants, and use a mask or face covering when working with fungi to avoid inhaling spores.

4. **Avoid uncertainty:** It is always safer to stick to what you know—especially when you are in an actual survival situation where your life is at

risk. Do not waste time and energy seeking out new types of foods if you have access to something that is familiar.

5. **Experiment only when you can afford to:** Experimentation while out foraging is undoubtedly important and has its place but only at the right time and in the right places. Ensure that you can get access to medical attention as soon as possible if something goes wrong.

6. **Memorize the locals:** Having a short list of safe foods to forage for in your area can help save you time and energy. List some useful plants, fungi, and easy-to-find animal resources like insects or bird nests.

7. **Consult an expert:** Foraging often involves using knowledge and information that is passed down through several generations and thoroughly tested to ensure its safety. Use this information to your advantage: Speak to the experts in your area or consult their books and videos before you begin a trek.

8. **Wash your food:** Removing any dirt and grime from your forage will make them more palatable, easier to prepare, and less likely to make you sick.

9. **Cook the food:** It is best to cook your foraged

foods wherever possible. This is important for plants, fungi, and animals. Wild animals are rife with parasites such as tapeworms, intestinal flukes, and toxoplasmosis which can cause havoc to your health if they are not killed before ingesting. Cooking is also important, as it makes most foods easier to digest, requiring less energy.

10. **Test new foods and ingest them in small quantities:** When experimenting or faced with a situation where you have no choice, you may encounter new foods. It is critical to carry out an edibility test first.

11. **Forage sustainably:** Only take what you need and avoid overharvesting. Harvest plants so that they stand a chance of recovering and reproducing and try to choose animals that are not in their breeding prime. Never collect endangered or rare species unless necessary for your survival: Even in the most severe circumstances, you may still face fines or prosecution under different laws.

12. **Know which parts of a plant you can eat:** Different parts of different plants will have different qualities. Some plants may have nutritious leaves but poisonous berries, while others have tasty roots below the surface but

toxic stems above. Selecting the correct parts of the plant and appropriately preparing them can make even some of the most treacherous plants safe for consumption.

13. **Harvest based on the season:** Certain parts of a plant will be the most nutritious during certain seasons. Spring is usually a sparse season with very little to eat. Fall is the time when many plants and animals prepare for the winter by storing nutrients, making them ripe for the picking. Leaves are generally most nutritious before the buds develop, flowers are most nutritious before any fruit or seeds begin to grow, and roots are most nutritious right before the winter.

14. **Plants can kill:** Do not underestimate the toxicity of certain plants. Poison hemlock, pokeweed, nettle, blue flag iris, and buckthorn are just some of the plants you may encounter that could easily lead to death if ingested. (Several poisonous plants are used by Indigenous people for medicinal purposes but involve supervision by experienced traditional practitioners and should not be imitated.)

15. **Most insects are safe to eat:** Insects are distinguished by having three pairs of legs, one pair of antennae, and three-segmented bodies.

Termites, grasshoppers, crickets, beetles, caterpillars, and bugs are excellent protein sources while foraging. It is best to avoid other creepy crawlies such as arachnids, scorpions, millipedes, and centipedes which can be venomous or poisonous.

16. **Bright colors are a warning:** Many animals, especially insects and even some plants, use bright, flashy colors to deter predators from eating them. It is usually a good indication that they contain poison or venom. The use of red, yellow, white, or black is most common.

17. **Do not shy away from slime:** Mollusks, like slugs, snails, and worms may seem off-putting, but there is usually nothing wrong with eating them if they are thoroughly cooked. (It is important to avoid bright coloration, though.)

18. **Small animals are better than no animals:** The thought of hunting large prey is exciting but challenging. Small animals such as birds, snakes, amphibians, and even rodents make for more manageable prey. They just need to be prepared with care by removing the skin/feathers and cooking thoroughly.

19. **Do not eat sickly plants, animals, or fungi:** Avoid eating plants or fungi that have discoloration, markings, or look wilted and

unhealthy in any way. Similarly, do not eat sick animals or those that have died from disease or infection.

20. **Avoid contaminated areas:** One of the major purposes of foraging is to get in touch with nature, and you should try to avoid human influences on the world, such as pollution. Do not harvest plants near power stations, from polluted rivers, near dumping sites, or other contaminated areas.

21. **An ocean of abundance:** Seas are a critical food source for coastal foragers, offering fish, sea vegetables, squid, octopus, and easy-to-collect animals like snails, starfish, and sea urchins.

22. **Vitamins and minerals are essential, too:** Ensuring you can forage for enough calories is only half of the task. It is also important to get a wide range of vitamins and minerals to maintain all the functions in your body. The water-soluble vitamins such as C and the Bs will quickly deplete, whereas fat-soluble vitamins like A, D, E, and K will be stored for longer periods.

23. **Do not trespass:** This rule is quite self-explanatory; nobody wants to end up in a jail cell—or worse, shot—by trespassing illegally on private land. Foraging is also banned in certain

national parks and protected areas, and it is best to consult with the rules and regulations beforehand.

24. **Share your knowledge so that others may enjoy foraging, too:** A major component of survivalism is ensuring that as many people can survive as possible. Not only this but helping more people to appreciate and participate in nature will lead them to protect and serve the natural world—helping to ensure a better and more secure future for the environment.

WHAT CAN YOU FORAGE?

In nature, there are certain types of foods that are more highly prized than others, primarily since they are more nutrient-dense or calorie-dense. Nutrient-dense foods have a large volume of nutrients per calorie, and calorie-dense foods offer more calories per weight. It is important to try and choose these kinds of foods whenever possible because you will need less of it to get a sufficient amount of nutrients and calories. Edible foods are rarely found in abundance in natural environments, and going hungry will be common. These foods will do little to fight hunger, but they will stave off starvation.

Another important aspect to note is that it is near impossible to survive on foraged plants alone for any extended amount of time. If you venture out into the wilderness, you will need to rely on animal foods to ensure you get enough calories and proteins. However, there are some esteemed plant foods that will definitely help:

Tree Nuts

Nuts are often produced in abundance by various trees during fall and can last long into the winter. They are dry fruits protected by a hard outer shell and are rich in proteins, fats, essential vitamins, and minerals. Most types take little to no preparation once you get the shells open, while others simply need to be boiled for a few minutes. Some of the best types of nuts to look out for are black walnuts, butternuts (white walnuts), hickory nuts, acorns, hazelnuts, chestnuts, beechnuts, pine nuts, and pecans.

Seeds

Seeds make another excellent source of food while out foraging. Several types of grasses and wildflowers produce edible seeds, supplying important minerals like calcium and iron along with satiating fats and protein. They will generally require some winnowing, milling, or grinding to break down the seed hull but can then be used to produce nourishing meal and porridges. Amaranth, curly dock, and lamb's quarters are favorites among foragers due to their relatively good yields and low processing requirements.

Roots and Tubers

Many plants store nutrients and minerals in their roots, forming large, edible tubers. These are usually a good source of carbohydrates such as starch and are easy to collect and prepare. Cattails, arrowroot, chicory, burdock, wild carrots, kudzu, and wild yams produce sizable and tasty tubers. Dandelions, blue thistle, daylilies, amaranth, and agave grow smaller but still edible roots. Roots can also include rhizomes; these are not technically root structures but instead are horizontal stems used by plants to spread and propagate. Rhizomes most commonly grow underground.

Berries and Fruit

Plants grow fruits so that they can be eaten! That is their entire purpose. They evolve to be as delicious, attractive, and tasty as possible so that foragers will keep coming back year after year. By eating the fruit, the seeds inside can be dispersed throughout the environment in the poop of various animals. Some kinds of seeds will never germinate unless they pass through a digestive tract. Berries such as raspberries, blackberries, blueberries, strawberries, and mulberries are among the most common types of fruit you are likely to encounter in the wild. Stone fruits, such as cherries, peaches, nectarines, mangoes, and avocados, are a little less common. They are an excellent source of vitamin C, K, E, and B vitamins.

FORAGING COMMON EDIBLES

Hunger is a good thing; it is a healthy and necessary feeling. Hunger stimulates the body and promotes an optimal metabolism. But there is a world of difference between feeling hungry and true starvation, and a small incident can trigger a chain of events that may quickly lead you down the path of starvation in a survival situation. With a dwindling food supply and aching stomach, it is essential that you are able to sustain yourself in the wilderness. Being able to identify some of the most common wild edibles can save you—buying you enough time to make it back to civilization.

These are among the most common edible plants that you may find in the wild. They occur naturally or have been introduced as useful species in North America and Europe; are easy to identify; and can serve as a useful food source for any beginner forager:

1. Prickly pear is an unmistakable cactus with large, spongy, paddle-shaped pads and deep pink fruits. There are no similar plants to mistake it for. The leaves and fruit are edible, including the seeds. They can be tricky to harvest, being covered in large spines and tiny bristles, but you just need to wear gloves and remove the fleshy leathery with a knife. The leaves can be eaten raw or cooked, but the fruits can be eaten fresh off the plant. Just one cup of the pads will provide about 14 calories, 20 mcg of vitamin A, 8 mg of vitamin C, 141 mg of calcium, and 5 mcg of vitamin K. One ripe prickly pear provides 42 calories with 10 g of carbohydrates, over 200 mg of potassium, and a good amount of vitamin C.

2. Morels are an earthy, nutty fungus that is relatively easy to identify. The cap can be spherical or pointed, but it has a regular shape with distinctive, undulating pits and ridges. The cap must be hollow and attach directly to the stem. False morels are a similar looking but highly poisonous relative: You can tell them apart because false morels are not hollow inside the cap. Morels can range in color from white to dark brown or blackish. They can be eaten raw or cooked. Just one cup worth of morel mushrooms can provide up to 20 calories and can meet up to half your daily iron requirements.

3. Chickweed is an annual and leafy plant that grows in large, tangled mats close to the ground. It has smooth, oblong, bright green leaves and small flowers with five pairs of tiny white petals. Chickweed leaves and stems make a helpful addition to a forager's diet, and the plant usually grows in abundance where it occurs. They do not offer much in calories but supplement the diet with ample fiber, vitamin A, vitamin C, B vitamins, iron, calcium, and potassium.

4. Dandelion is a common weed with long, toothy, and notched leaves that grow in a whorl on the ground. Dandelions are tough and can be found in most environments. They produce large yellow flowers that develop into fluffy blowballs. All parts of a dandelion can be eaten, but the leaves are most prized—they can be cooked like spinach or eaten raw. The greens can provide up to 45 calories from only 100 g, supplying half the daily requirements of vitamin A, up to 35 mg of vitamin C, and several times the necessary amount of vitamin K. They are also rich in manganese, iron, copper, and calcium. Dandelions have served people for thousands of years and in recent times—during the Great Depression, many families were able to manage by eating the dandelions growing in streets and parks.

5. Raspberries and Blackberries are a true delicacy of nature. These berries grow on trees and bushes and are safe to eat. They have a unique appearance with no similar kinds to worry about. These berries grow in tight clusters of several tiny individual sacs filled with juice, and raspberries are generally hollow inside. A cup of raspberries or blackberries can provide more than 60 calories, half your daily vitamin C requirements, and good amounts of various other vitamins and minerals to supplement your diet.

6. Blueberries are equally as tasty as blueberries or raspberries. Blueberries can provide critical nutrients but carry the risk of misidentification. Several poisonous plants grow berries resembling blueberries, including ivy, nightshade, pokeweed, and Virginia creepers. Blueberries are identified by their protruding five-pointed crown, waxy blue-purple skin, and light flesh growing from thin green stems on bushes. A close relative, the bilberry, is similar but smaller, though they are also edible and not a concern for poisoning. A serving of 100 g of blueberries can provide nearly 60 calories, and they are rich in vitamin C, vitamin K1, and manganese.

7. **Chicken of the woods** is a great mushroom for beginner foragers due to its bright color. It is said to taste like chicken! This mushroom can be found growing on the sides of hardwood trees like oak, cherry, or beech. It is distinguished by other yellow or orange mushrooms by the underside and covered in tiny pores, not gills (a slightly similar mushroom is the jack-o'-lantern which has gills on the underside). Chicken of the woods should be harvested quite young

to ensure a soft, pliable texture and cooked thoroughly. Just 100 g of the fungus can provide 14 g of protein and about 25 calories. It is a good source of potassium, vitamin C, and vitamin A as well.

8. **Amaranths** are erect, broad-leafed plants with long spikes covered in bright pink, purple, or crimson flowers. The flowers develop numerous tiny white seeds which are edible, but the leaves and stems are also suit-

able for eating. The greens can offer nearly 30 calories and are rich in vitamin K, vitamin C, calcium, iron, manganese, and magnesium. A serving of 100 g of seeds contains about 370 calories and is also very high in manganese, phosphorus, magnesium, copper, iron, and selenium. Both the seeds and the greens must be thoroughly cooked—usually by boiling.

9. Cattails are a common feature in wetlands and near streams or lakes; cattails make for a valuable source of carbohydrates. The young shoots and roots are edible, though people have also turned to the sausage-like flowers during famines. The roots can be dried and ground down into flour or boiled like other tubers. They are rich in starchy carbohydrates, while the stalks provide vitamins A, B, and C, potassium, and phosphorus.

10. Chanterelle is a mushroom that grows on forest floors with its distinctive yellow-orange coloration. It can provide a delicious addition to a forager's diet with peppery notes and a light and fruity taste. Chanterelles are easy to identify, having forked gills on the underside and a flared trumpet shape. The only similar mushroom is the jack-o'-lantern which differs by growing in groups on trees. Chanterelles grow individually; they are creamy white when cut open and smell fruity, like apricots. A cup of wild chanterelles have about 18 calories but is high in vitamin D, iron, copper, vitamin B3, and B5. They can be eaten raw or cooked.

WHERE TO FIND YOUR EDIBLES

You now have an idea of what to look out for while foraging—great! But where do you even begin? You may be surprised to learn that many of these plants are incredibly tenacious and thrive in almost any environment. Dandelions are a good example—growing in wild habitats, cities, and urban areas—exploiting the cracks in paving and waste disposal sites. Several of the most common edible species have been introduced throughout the world, primarily due to their beneficial medicinal and nutritional properties. You don't really need to venture out into the woods to find several of these plants. Your gardens, parks, vacant lots, and sidewalks are an excellent place to begin foraging before you head out into the wilderness. Prickly pears, native to the deserts of Central America, can grow well in almost any habitat and are even found along roadsides.

When you do find yourself in a wild environment, there are some tips and tricks that can increase your foraging yields:

- Plants need access to water, especially in drier climates, so it is best to begin by seeking out waterways which will inevitably lead you to various different kinds of plants.
- In regions without surface water, plants will try to access the groundwater. This is common in large, open spaces where you may find a few small outcrops of trees that have managed to dig down below the surface into aquifers. These outcrops will attract opportunistic species that may be edible.
- In humid climates, access to water will not be a problem, and edible plants are more likely to be found in open areas and clearings with lots of sunshine.
- In humid climates, rocky outcrops are also an excellent place to look. The rocks provide good drainage and prevent plants from getting waterlogged, making them an ideal habitat.
- The edges of a forest are a good place to look

for plants because they gain protection from strong winds, allowing them to grow better.

- The bases of hardwood trees and their surrounding areas are the best place to find various kinds of edible mushrooms.

- In general, plants that grow in abundance are more likely to be edible. This is because their seeds are more likely to be dispersed by various animals that feed on them. Animals will tend to avoid toxic varieties, and it is more difficult for them to be dispersed.

CONCLUSION

"Study nature, love nature, stay close to nature. It will never fail you."

— FRANK LLOYD WRIGHT

Knowing how to safely and efficiently forage for wild, edible plants is not only a fun skill. It can help save your life in a difficult situation, save you money by offering you more food choices, and it is built upon an ancient tradition that helped our species survive. Foraging connects one with nature in a way that few other skills can.

However, you do not need to find yourself in a survival situation to begin. Some of the best places to begin honing your skills are on your own land or in your local parks and green spaces. You will find several herbs, berries, roots, and other edible plant foods which have found their way into urban spaces. It is also a great way for you to begin learning how to collect, store, and preserve plants for future use. Keep an eye out near agricultural areas, livestock pastures, and fields where you may find plants such as sunflowers, plantain, thistle, or Jerusalem artichokes. Visit rivers and streams to investigate the aquatic plants—cattails, watercress, water pepper, wasabi, and lotus to name a few. Just keep in mind that pollution is a factor in urban environments, and most plants are likely to be contaminated to some degree by industrial fertilizers or pesticides, along with particulate matter and heavy metals.

2

PLANT IDENTIFICATION AND SAFETY

P lant identification is a significant component of foraging, and being able to identify and discern between edible and poison varieties is critical. Several plants have close relatives with similar appearances but different chemical properties. While one may make a nutritious addition to a salad, the other could lead to seizures and paralysis.

I can share my own experience of preventing my friend from consuming what he thought was a safe plant. While hiking and exploring in the woodlands, my friend spotted some enticing berries resembling wild grapes. They were the right size, shape, and color: 1 cm (0.39 inches) in diameter, round, and blue-black. He handed some to me before eating them, and I quickly opened the flesh up to find the ominous crescent-shaped seed indicating that these were not wild grapes but the highly poisonous fruits of the Canadian moonseed plant. Luckily, neither he nor I had eaten any of the berries yet. We would expect to experience stomach pain, dizziness, and nausea, followed by convulsions and possibly death. Unfortunately, far too many foragers have managed to poison themselves by consuming toxic lookalikes, and many have died because of it. By following the forager's rules, you can avoid these risks.

PATTERNS IN NATURE

"There are patterns in everything, in the whole of Nature, from the way the stars turn in the heavens to the whorl of a shell or the petals of a flower and the way leaves arrange themselves about a twig."

— CELIA REES

Nature loves patterns. Being able to identify these patterns is a skill at which the human brain is incredibly adept. All living things can be grouped and classified based on their similarities and differences. We distinguish between flowering plants and cone-producing plants; between vascular plants and nonvascular plants; between trees, shrubs, bushes, and thickets; between the different shapes and margins of leaves; and between the types of roots growing below the ground. Similar plants will have similar patterns or characteristics because they are related. Generally, the more closely related two plants are, the more patterns they will have in common. This includes not only their appearances but also their edibility, nutrient, and medicinal properties.

PLANT IDENTIFICATION BASICS

Botanical Terminology

It will save you a lot of time and effort to familiarize yourself with some of the most common botanical terminology. This will help you to understand the differences and similarities between plants and make for quicker, more reliable identification.

Botanical Glossary of Terms

- Alternate: Leaves alternating back and forth on either side of a stem
- Bipinnate: A leaf that is split in two orders of leaflets so that each leaflet is also composed of leaflets
- Compound Leaf: A single leaf broken up into

several smaller leaflets, e.g. pinnate
- Evergreen: A plant, usually trees, that keep their leaves during winter
- Lobed: Leaves with deeply indented margins
- Midrib: The central vein of a leaf
- Node: The point along a stem where leaves or branches grow
- Opposite: Leaves grow in pairs on opposite sides of a stem
- Pinnate: A leaf that is split into one order of leaflets
- Pistil: The female reproductive part of a flower made up of the ovary, the tube called the style, and the sticky tip called the stigma
- Raceme: An arrangement of flowers where individuals grow on short stalks at equal distances along the length of a stem
- Rhizome: An underground stem that grows horizontally and resembles a root
- Rosette: A tight circular ring of leaves or leaflets
- Serrated margin: A leaf with edges that have forward-pointing teeth
- Stamen: The male reproductive part of a flower made of a stalk called the filament and the tip called the anther
- Toothed margin: A leaf with edges that have sharp indentations

Plant Families

Most plants are easily categorized into different families. This includes the following:

The Conifer Family

Known scientifically as *Pinaceae*, conifers include evergreen, softwood trees with scale- or needle-like leaves and reproduce cones to reproduce. Conifer trees are much older than any of the flowering plants and are most commonly found in cooler regions around the world. Conifers include cedar, cypress, Douglas fir, fir, juniper, larch, pine, redwood, spruce, and yew trees. Most parts of conifer trees are not edible, but some produce nutritious nuts in the scales of their cones.

The Daisy Family

Also known as the sunflower family or *Asteraceae*, these plants are characterized by their compound flowers made up of disk florets and ray florets. They include sunflowers, daisies, chrysanthemums, dandelions, thistles, dahlias, cosmos, chamomile, feverfew, burdock, and artichoke. The compound flower head may appear as one single flower but is actually composed of several very small and modified "florets." The disk florets often form a central, flat disk shape while the ray florets form the outer ring of colorful petals. However, sometimes the two types of florets look very similar.

The Grass Family

Grasses, known as *Poaceae* or *Gramineae*, are a specialized type of flowering plant adapted to living in drier climates and rely on the wind for seed dispersal. Grasses include cereals, bamboo, cattails, and reeds. All grains are grasses—barley, corn, oats, rice, millet, rye, sorghum, and wheat. Sugarcane is another economically significant grass, along with the various varieties of ornamental and lawn grasses. Grasses grow as unbranching erect stems called culms which are round in shape, compared to sedges or rushes which are angular. They have nodes separating different segments up the stem and often develop extensive underground stems called rhizomes.

The Fern Family

Ferns are among the oldest of all living vascular plants which means they use specialized conductive tissues to transport water, minerals, and nutrients. They are also nonflowering, reproducing using spores that generally rely on water to disperse them. Ferns include many different kinds of plants, including the traditional fern, club mosses, and horsetails—which commonly occur in moist forests. Most of these plants are not valued as a food source; however, the young fiddleheads of various ferns and the tender stems of horsetails are edible.

The Mint Family

Plants from the mint family—*Lamiaceae*—are among the easiest to identify and forage. They are flowering plants that include mint, rosemary, oregano, sage, thyme, basil, marjoram, and lavender. Mint plants are herbaceous, meaning they do not have woody stems, their leaves are highly aromatic, they have square stems which you can feel when you roll them between your fingers, and the leaves grow in pairs on opposite sides of the branches. Nearly all species in the mint family— of which there are over 3,000—are edible. They do not provide many calories but can be used to spice and flavor foods and offer up essential nutrients and minerals.

The Mustard Family

Mustard plants from the *Brassicaceae* family include a number of common cruciferous vegetables such as broccoli, cauliflower, watercress, mustard greens, turnips, kale, arugula, radishes, collard greens, and rutabaga. They are best distinguished by their flowers, which have four petals arranged in either an X- or an H-shape, and six stamens, of which two will be short and four will be tall. The flowers grow on a raceme. (Most cruciferous vegetables result from extensive selective breeding that has modified the flowers, making these identification criteria useless; however, if you stumble across broccoli in the wild, rest assured that you can eat it.)

The Parsley Family

Apiaceae, or *Umbelliferae,* also called the carrot or celery family, includes parsley, celery, carrots, angelica, anise, caraway, coriander, cumin, dill, fennel, and parsnips. It also includes several poisonous species such as poison hemlock, spotted cowbane, water dropwort, and fool's parsley. One of the main features in the parsley family is the compound umbels. Umbels are a type of flower structure where a single stem gives rise to several small flower stalks originating from the same point, like the ribs of an umbrella. They are compound because each flower stalk gives rise to several small flowers which sometimes appear as a single unit. The flower stalks of parsley plants are usually hollow and they have lacy, compound leaves that are divided and lobed into smaller leaflets.

The Pea Family

Also known as the legume family or *Fabaceae*, plants from the pea family include acacia, alfalfa, beans, clover, cowpea, fenugreek, lentils, licorice, peas, peanuts, and soybeans. They include herbaceous and woody plants ranging in size from small shrubs to large trees. They have unique flowers making them easy to identify: Each flower has five petals—one large petal forming the "banner," two slightly smaller lateral petals forming the "wings," and two much smaller, fused petals called the "keel" which encase the sepals and style. Their seeds develop in pods which can be fleshy or dry, and they usually have pinnate leaves—a leaf is split into small leaflets which grow on either side of the midrib.

WHAT TO EAT AND WHAT NOT TO EAT

Remember: Plants can kill you. Even a small handful of the Canadian moonseed berries I mentioned earlier could have taken down a full-grown man. By following some simple identification rules, you can easily avoid such situations:

- Plants growing in urban areas are almost always contaminated with pesticides or fertilizer and should be washed thoroughly before consumption.
- Some contaminants are absorbed by the plant and cannot be removed. This can include plants growing near industrial waste sites and mines.
- Even plants growing in natural environments may be contaminated—parasites such as *Giardia* are found in waterways, and *E. coli* occurs in animal feces. Wash and boil your food before eating.
- Many plants produce toxic amounts of cyanide which can depend on the environment in which they grow. A plant from one region may be safe, but the same species in another region may not be. Avoid cyanide by looking out for a strong almond-like smell.
- Know yourself: Many people have sensitive

digestive systems. You may be prone to bloating, indigestion, constipation, or diarrhea from typical, store-bought foods. If that is the case, foraging for wild foods is probably not a good option.

- If you are particularly sensitive to poison ivy, you should avoid all sumac plants while foraging, resulting in similar reactions. This can include cashews, plums, mango, pistachio, sugar bush, and poison oak.
- Some plants are high in bitter-tasting tannins and can cause acid reflux. They can be removed by cooking your food.
- Some plants are high in oxalates which can lead to kidney damage for some people. Oxalates can also be destroyed by cooking.
- When in doubt, conduct a universal edibility test first.

Universal Edibility Test

This test is best for unidentified plants that you can find in abundance. It is a waste of your time to go through this entire process if you cannot access a large enough volume of the plant to sustain you in the first place. It takes more than 24 hours to test one part of a plant, and you will often need to test many different parts of the plant consecutively.

1. The first step is to separate the plant into its different parts—roots, stems, leaves, buds, and flowers.

2. You should only work with one part of the plant at a time. (Flowers may be edible but leaves may not, and if you test both parts at the same time, your results will be unclear.)

3. Smell the plant for strong or unpleasant odors. If you detect an almond smell, do not eat this part of the plant; however, various other smells do not necessarily mean it is inedible. Keep a mental note of this information.

4. It is best to conduct the test on an empty stomach—do not eat for at least eight hours prior. You should use this time to carry out other tasks that are essential for your survival such as finding water, setting up a shelter, and collecting firewood.

5. The skin test: Take a small piece of the plant and place it onto the thin skin of your wrist or inner elbow for up to 15 minutes. If you notice any irritation, burning, numbness, redness, etc., then you know that you should not eat this part of the plant.

6. If the part of the plant passes the skin test, you can proceed to the next step.

7. Prepare the part of the plant in the way you

plan to eat it. Make sure to wash it thoroughly before boiling or cooking over a fire. Then, rub the cooked plant onto your lips and wait about 15 minutes to see if there is a reaction. If you notice any irritation, burning, numbness, redness, etc., then you should not eat this part of the plant.

8. If there is no reaction, take a small bite of the cooked plant and chew it, but do not swallow. Hold it in your mouth for about 15 minutes to see if there is a reaction. Also look out for any bitterness or soapy tastes. If you have a bad reaction, then you shouldn't eat this part of the plant.

9. If the plant passes this part of the test, swallow the small piece and wait about eight hours for your body to digest it. Look out for serious side effects like vomiting, nausea, or diarrhea as well as milder side effects like stomach pains or aches. (Eating any foreign foods on an empty stomach can lead to some discomfort, so take this into account.)

10. If there are ill effects, try to rid your body of the plant materials by inducing vomiting and drinking lots of water.

11. If there are no ill effects, then you can consider this part of the plant safe to eat and consume it

in larger quantities. Try to eat less than ¼ cup at a time just in case there are some poisonous properties that are only noticeable in larger doses.

12. The other parts of the plant should all be tested in the same way if you would like to try and eat them.

13. You should only eat these plant parts when they are prepared in the same way as during the test.

Common Look-Alikes

Know the most common look-alikes and refer to a plant identification guide if in doubt:

Edible Plant	Poisonous Look-alike
sweet almonds	bitter almonds
wild grapes	Canadian moonseed (or 'fox grapes')
true morels	false morels
wild carrot and parsnip	hemlock
wild garlic	death camas, lilies, and false garlic
wild tomatoes	horse nettles, bittersweet nightshade
black nightshade	deadly nightshade
wild cherries	buckthorn
bay leaf	rhododendrons
staghorn and red-berried sumac	poison sumac
grapevine	Virginia creeper
young cattails	blue iris

What NOT to Eat While Foraging

Poisonous and inedible plants will share many common features that are easy to remember. You should try to avoid these types of plants:

- Sickly looking plants: anything with mold, mildew, black spots, blight, or cankers on any part of the plant
- Plants that smell of almonds
- Plants with milky or colored sap (Dandelion is a rare exception.)
- Most legumes, beans, seed pods, and bulbs
- White or yellow berries
- Most plants with thorns, spines, or fine hairs
- Most plants in the parsley family with umbrella-shaped flowers and lacy leaves
- Grass grains that have black, pink, or purple spurs
- Most plants with three-compound leaves.
- Mushrooms: Few mushrooms are safe to eat, and it is very risky to eat any that you find in the wild. Only eat mushrooms if you are 100% certain of their species, and you can access immediate medical attention if necessary.

3

BUILDING A FIRE

The ability to control fire is considered a major factor in the evolution of our species—cooked foods contributed to the explosive development of our large brains which could be fueled with the more readily digestible and palatable foods. Fire also reduced the occurrence of intestinal parasites and disease which allowed early man to venture out into colder climates in the Northern Hemisphere. The comfort brought on by a fire is a primal instinct instilled in all of us.

Knowing how to build a fire in many different situations is one of the most important skills of a survivalist. Fire is used to disinfect water of pathogens and bacteria; to disinfect plant and animal foods; to cook foods and make them edible; and also keep you warm. Fire is also a great defense against wild animals and biting insects.

PREPPING A FIREPLACE

First, you will need a safe area in which to build the fire:

- It should be a good distance—15 to 30 feet— away from the rest of your campsite.
- Your fire should always be downwind of your campsite.
- The area should be clear of flammable debris like plant material, especially dry grass. This also includes treetops and branches above the fire.
- Choose an area with bare soil, sand, or gravel.
- Bank for your fire using a ring of rocks. (Rocks saturated with water can explode under high heat, so choose dry rocks.)
- Dig a shallow pit in the center to concentrate your coals and reduce smoke.

GATHERING MATERIALS

Before you can build a fire, you need to gather and prepare all the necessary materials:

- Tinder: This is very fine, dry, and highly flammable material used to catch a spark and ignite a small flame. It can include dry leaves, bark, wood shavings, dry grass, moss, and even twine, cotton balls, newspaper shreds, or dryer lint.

- Kindling: This is a slightly larger flammable material used to fuel the small flames in the tinder. The best types of kindling are very small, thin branches and twigs which are dry enough to snap. Kindling should be added to the fire in stages, from the smallest pieces to progressively larger ones, until the small fire is raging happily.

- Firewood: These are large pieces of wood that will burn slowly and fuel the fire for long periods. You can use branches, logs, and pine cones from any tree. Softwood trees like conifers will burn more quickly and at higher temperatures, whereas hardwood burns more slowly. The firewood does not have to be completely dry for the fire to burn properly, though drier woods are always preferred.

FIRE DESIGN

Once you have collected all the materials, you can begin putting the fire together. There are a few different fire designs, each suited to different purposes, which we will discuss below:

- **Teepee:** This design is the most common way to build a fire. First, lay down a bed of tinder and then sit up your kindling in a teepee shape, tapering to a point at the top. As the fire begins to burn more strongly, you can add larger pieces of firewood to the outside of the structure. The firewood should not be packed too tightly as to restrict airflow—especially when coals and embers begin to collect in the center. Teepee fires are good for warming you up quickly, as they burn through wood hot and fast. You need to place additional pieces of firewood up against the sides, making it an easy design to maintain.

- **Log cabin:** This design is another simple arrangement beginning with a bed of tinder on which you can lay some pieces of kindling down flat, all in a similar direction. Once you have a flame going, begin laying down two to three pieces of firewood parallel to each other. Build another layer in the direction perpendicular to the base, and repeat this process until the fire is as big as you need it to be. You can also build the entire structure and then ignite it at the base to avoid burning yourself. There should be spaces in between each piece of firewood to allow for airflow. This type of design burns more slowly than a teepee and is good if you need the fire to last a long time.

- **Upside down:** This design is similar to the log cabin except the purpose is to ignite it from tinder and kindling at the top rather than the base. This allows a bed of coals to form, on which pots or pans can be placed for cooking food. It is also a relatively slow-burning method but can build up a lot of heat due to the bed of coals in the center.

- **Lean-to:** This type of fire uses the wood as a windbreak and can be used to cook foods in windy conditions. Use a relatively large piece of firewood and lay it on its side. Set up a small bed of tinder and kindling on the downwind side so that it is protected. Ignite the fire and lay smaller pieces of firewood on top so that their tips lean on the large piece. The smaller pieces of firewood should burn through and be replaced before the larger piece. This method is not very good for warming spaces but can be used to cook foods.

- **Star:** This design is good for when you don't have a lot of firewood to work with. Set up a bed of tinder and kindling in the center of a firepit and lay your pieces of firewood in a star shape with the tips pointing inward. Ignite the fire, and it will burn only the tips. You can maintain the fire by pushing the logs inward toward the center when needed. You can also salvage the rest of the unburned firewood using this method.
- **Self-Feeding:** This design is a bit more complex but is good if you are busy working on other tasks and need the fire to continue burning with minimal maintenance. You will need to build a large support frame in the shape of a V so that logs can be stacked onto the diagonal frames and roll down into the center as logs burn out. The frame must be large enough to avoid direct contact with the flames.

FLAME TO FIRE

Starting a fire without matches or a lighter can be a frustrating or exciting challenge. There are several traditional methods you should try, but there are a few modern hacks that you can use to get your fires started:

- The Hand Drill: This method uses friction to create a tiny glowing ember which can be transferred to a bed of tinder. It takes quite a lot of elbow grease and can be quite an exhausting method—not ideal when you are running low on calories. Still, it is a good skill to have in your arsenal:
- You will need a long, straight, and smooth stick —the drill—and a flatter piece of wood to serve as the fireboard.
- The tip of the drill stick must be carved into a point, and a notch must be cut into the center of the fireboard for the drill tip to sit in.
- It is helpful to create a small bed of tinder right next to this notch.
- To create friction, you need to spin the stick in between your hands as you apply downward pressure.
- Keep repeating this until you see a small amount of smoke. Then, you can begin looking for a tiny, glowing ember.
- Feed the ember with a small amount of tinder and allow the small fire to grow and develop. Then transfer it to a fireplace with some tinder, adding successively larger pieces.

The Fire Plow: This is very similar to the hand drill except your fireboard will have a long groove running lengthwise. This method works best if you use a hardwood stick and softwood fireboard, as the purpose is to create fine, heated shavings from the softwood:

- Use your hardwood stick to rub up and down within the groove of the fireboard rapidly.
- A small pile of tinder will begin to form at the edge of the fireboard beneath the groove.
- If you keep rubbing long and hard enough, you will be able to form an ember which can be fed with some fine tinder.
- Once the tinder is lit, transfer it to a fire pit

where you can feed it with kindling and then pieces of firewood.

The Bow Drill: This method also uses friction but instead of having to use your hands to spin the drill stick, it's a bow with string or twine. It is a much more efficient method if you have some kind of string, twine, or shoelace available:

- The bow should be about as long as your arm to improve efficiency.
- The string of the bow must be looped around the drill stick so that when you move it back and forth, the drill stick will spin.
- Place the tip of the drill stick into the fireboard the same as in the previously mentioned methods.
- You can also use a support board on the top of the drill stick as shown in the image below.
- Draw the bow back and forth while applying downward pressure to the drill stick.
- Wait until you see a small amount of smoke and look out for a glowing ember.
- Feed the ember with a small amount of tinder. Once the tinder is lit, feed it with kindling and transfer it to a fire pit.

These are some of the most traditional and primitive methods of starting a fire. However, in the modern world, we have access to a variety of other types of materials that could be useful and save you time and energy:

- **Flint and steel:** A flint stick is a common tool in many survivalist's tool kits. Flint is a type of rock which, when struck with steel, will create a hot spark. You can use these sparks to ignite a small bed of tinder.
- **Lenses:** Lenses can be constructed using several

types of material, from actual lenses made from glass, the lenses in a pair of glasses, clear plastic bags filled with water, or even ice. As long as the materials can be used to refract water, you can direct the sunlight into a small beam which can be used to heat up and ignite tinder.

- **Mirrors:** There are several objects that reflect light well. One example is polishing the base of a soda can with fine sand or even chocolate. Reflecting and directing sunlight onto a bed of tinder can work to ignite it if you are patient.

- **Electricity:** If you have access to a battery, making a fire can be an easy task. All you will need is a type of conductive metal to connect the two terminals of the battery together. This includes copper, silver, gold, aluminum, and some alloys like steel. This should work to heat up the metal enough to ignite fine pieces of tinder. A rectangular nine-volt battery works best for this method.

PLANTS TO COOK

There are several wild plants that should be cooked before eating. This can work to not only disinfect them but also destroy several harmful compounds, like tannins or oxalates, and make them more palatable and easier to digest.

- **Clovers:** All parts of a clover plant can be eaten, from the roots to the flowers, and they often grow in abundance. White clover is usually the most prized, but all species are edible. The roots, stems, leaves, and flowers should be boiled first, but you can also fry or roast them.

- **Nettles:** Cooking destroys the stinging hairs that cover the leaves and stems of nettles, making them safe to eat. The young shoots and leaves are the best for eating, as they are the most tender. Boil them, discard the used water, and rinse them once more before eating. Remember to handle the raw plant with gloves.

- **Oak:** The acorns produced by oak trees are
  edible if prepared, though they are highly
  astringent when raw. They will need to be
  deshelled and either soaked in water for about
  12 hours or boiled to remove the bitter
  compounds. While boiling them, it is often
  better to change the water a few times to ensure
  all the chemicals are removed.

- **Cattails:** There are many different parts of the cattail plant that can be eaten at different times of the year. The roots can be soaked in water to separate the starch from the fibers, and the starchy water makes a good addition for a stew or soup. The young shoots can be eaten raw, though more mature parts of the stem need to be boiled, fried, or roasted. The seed heads are highly nutritious, growing on the sausage shapes with feathery attachments. Strip the seeds away from the stem and winnow them to remove the chaff. This will leave behind only the kernels which should be boiled to soften them.

- **Violets:** The greens of violet plants can be
  boiled, stewed, or fried before eating. Younger
  leaves will be more tender than older leaves.
  The flower heads are also edible raw but can
  make a nice addition to an herbal tea.

- **Plantain:** Also known as broad-leaf plantain or plantain weed, this plant is not the same as the one that produces the banana-like fruit. It grows as a rosette of leaves close to the ground with erect stalks covered in seeds when mature. The leaves can be eaten raw when young but require boiling to make them tender and edible when they are older. The seeds can be collected from the stalks and winnowed before boiling them and using them in a stew or to make flour.

- **Kelp:** If you find yourself foraging near the ocean, keep an eye out for seaweed and kelp. All kinds are edible. It is best to dry them thoroughly first (which can be done using a fire or roasting them). You can then eat them in the dried form and incorporate them into a stew.

- **Bamboo:** The young shoots of bamboo are good for eating but can be quite tough. Cooking can help to make them more tender, either by boiling, frying or roasting. The shoots are usually small and conical, appearing close to the ground.

4

EMERGENCY COOKING

Now that you know how to build a fire, it is important to know how to cook in a survival situation. You need to be able to actually harvest and transport the foods back to your campsite, cut them up, winnow the seeds, mash the roots, and contain them in a vessel for cooking. You may not have access to baskets, bags, bottles, sharp knives, forks, spoons, pots, pans, and/or roasting trays.

Some of the most useful tools to have when foraging are the following:

- A basket or bag to carry your tools and foods in
- A digging stick to help access tubers and roots
- Gloves to protect your hands from stinging plants, spines, and thorns

- A sharp knife for cutting leaves, stems, and roots
- A large knife for chopping grasses, tough stems, and thickets
- An axe for cutting wood
- A container for transporting water
- A cooking container like a pot
- A plate or bowl from which to eat your food
- A weapon—both for defending against and hunting animals
- Rope for climbing or making pulleys
- Utensils like forks and spoons

However, if you find yourself needing to forage for survival, it is unlikely that you came prepared with all of these tools. Luckily, many can be obtained from nature.

MAKING TOOLS FROM NATURE

Nature can provide the materials to make almost any tool you may need.

Tools

Knife: One of the primary items that will be used to construct other tools is a knife. You should always try to carry a pocket knife with you when you go out into the wilderness; however, if you do find yourself without one, there is still hope. Just like our ancestors did, sharp blades can be produced using rocks.

- Find the ideal rocks in outcrops, streams, or creeks. The best types of rocks for this purpose are flint, chert, jasper, chalcedony, quartz, and obsidian, but you will need to test a few different types out to see what works best. You will need a reasonably large rock with lots of unweathered material inside.
- You will also need a round hammerstone with which to strike the rock and chip off pieces.
- Though optional, you may also want to use an anvil stone; this will help support the rock when you strike it, providing percussive resistance that can help produce shards. It must be a hard surface—not your lap or soft ground.

- Be careful when striking the hammerstone on the rock, as it can produce exceptionally sharp shards. Rocks like flint can produce cutting edges sharper than surgical blades. You can protect yourself by wrapping your hands in leaves.

- The purpose of stone knapping, in a survival situation, is not to shape a perfect blade from the rock. Instead, you should try to chip off smaller, sharp shards that can be used to cut. This will save you time and effort. Stone knapping is a tedious skill that takes years to master.

Axe: A primitive hand-axe can be produced in a similar way, though instead of using the small shards, you will focus on trying to shape an edge out of your large rock. It is important to keep a smooth surface at the back of the cutting edge, on which to place your hand. You can use it as a hand-axe or try to attach the head of the axe to a sturdy handle.

Rope: Ropes are made from plant fibers that are processed and wrapped. You can use the fibers from any plants that have long, stringy stems and stalks including hemp, cattails, stinging nettle, yucca, spruce, dogbane, or red cedar. You will need to cut the stalks and strip them of bark and soft inner material (which can be done by boiling them first). Then dry and buff them, though you can also find plant material that is already dry. Buffing the fibers involves beating the fibers to soften them and make them pliable. Then, you need to wrap the cords. There are a few different ways to do this. The simplest way is to get two or three bunches of fiber and twist them in one direction while wrapping them around each other in the opposite direction. You can scale this process up by starting with small cords and using those cords to make larger ropes.

Utensils

Forks and spoons: Once you have a knife or blade, you can easily cut branches and twigs from trees and carve them into the shape of primitive forks and spoons. It is best to strip the outer bark away before using them.

Bowls and plates: Wooden bowls and plates can be easily produced in nature:

- The easiest way to do this is to find a branch or small log and split it in half. Then, use hot coals to burn away at the insides. You can use a knife to help carve and scrape away the burned material. You need to do this until you create a cavity that is big enough for your purposes.
- However, bowls and plates can also be made using large plant leaves—banana leaves are ideal as they have a smooth, nontoxic surface; flat stones; or hollowed-out tree trunks.
- You can also create your own clay pots with a little practice. Clay is found in many moist habitats and can be shaped and formed into plates or bowls. You then need to bake them near a hot fire until they set and dry.

Water Containers

You can make containers for storing and transporting out of wood, bamboo, animal parts, or even coconut shells:

- You can carry water over short distances using wooden bowls produced using the methods described above.
- Bamboo makes for an excellent water carrier, as the stems are naturally hollow inside and have segments that are sealed. You just need to cut down a large stem to the size you need and clean out the insides.
- There are several plants that develop large seed pods, such as sausage trees or gourd vines. These seed pods can be hollowed out and dried to produce the perfect water container. Bottle gourds have been cultivated in many areas specifically for this purpose.

- Various parts of animals can be used to contain water, including their bladders, skin, and intestines. If you are able to catch a large enough animal for this purpose, you will need to thoroughly wash and scrape the linings of these tissues before using them.

Cooking Containers

It is critical to have a container that you can withstand the heat of boiling water:

- **Wooden bowls:** Though a wooden bowl cannot be placed directly over a fire to boil water, you can use hot rocks to boil water instead. Simply heat up some clean rocks in a fire and transfer them into the wooden bowl filled with water. You may need a few rocks and transfer them back and forth between the bowl and the fire a few times before it begins to boil. The same can be done with bamboo or a gourd, but this may damage them over time.

- **Tree stump:** You may be lucky enough to find a reasonably hollowed-out tree stump. Use hot coals to smooth out the surface before pouring your water inside. Then, you can use the same hot rock method described above to bring the water to a boil.

- **Waterskins:** The stomachs, hides, or intestines of animals can be used to bring water to a boil. You can suspend the containers above a fire. Due to the physics of water, it will never get hotter than 212 °F , and most animal tissues will be able to hold up well enough. Hot rocks may burn through these materials.

- **A large leaf** can be used to contain water when using the hot rock method or by suspending it over a fire.

- **Hole in the ground:** You can also dig out a hole in the ground, though this works better in soils with a high clay content. You can line the hole with rocks, clay, and grass to create a watertight surface, and use the hot rock method to bring the water to a boil. You may need to bake the surface using hot coals before adding water.

- **Trash:** It is difficult to escape man's impact on the world, and even in the most remote locations, it is likely that you will stumble upon trash such as plastic bottles, drink cans, and plastic bags. All of these can be used to boil water and cook foods. A plastic bag filled with water can safely be suspended above a fire without burning. Water boils at 212 °F and does not get hotter, whereas the plastic burns at higher temperatures. Plastic materials may warp, but this is not a problem as long as it contains your water. However, hot rocks may burn through these materials.

Weapons

Weapons are necessary tools for defense when you are out in the wild, but you will primarily use them to catch food. Some of the oldest weapons employed by humans include spears, atlatls, rock slings, and the bow and arrow.

- **Spears:** Making a spear is simple enough, though you can take them to the next level. Spears must be made from long, sturdy, and straight pieces of wood. You can sharpen the tips using a knife and then harden it in a fire until the end turns black. You can also add sharp stone blades to the tip by carving away some wood to create a "shelf" on which the blade can sit. Secure the blade using lashings made from string, twine, plastic, leather, or animal intestines.

- **Atlatl:** Also known as a spear-thrower, this tool can help increase the accuracy, range, and power of your spear throws, making them better suited to larger prey. They are made from thicker and heavier branches than you would use for spears—up to almost three inches in diameter but only about one-third the length. They have a spur on one end that connects to the butt of the spear. The spears may need to be altered to fit into the throwers.

- **Rock slings:** This is a very powerful and (with practice) deadly accurate weapon suited to small game like rabbits and birds but also good for fending off predators—think David and Goliath. A rock sling is made with any kind of cord, including leather, paracord, or rope. It needs to be about two to four feet long, depending on the reach of your arms. In the center is a small hammock in which rocks can sit. You use a rock sling by holding both ends in your hand and spinning the rock above your head, releasing one end when you are ready to hit a target.

- **Bow and arrow:** A classic piece of weaponry that can be difficult to master. It is best not to try and produce your own bow and arrow because it is quite an art form. There are several affordable models of bows, recurve bows, longbows, and crossbows in camping and survival stores that you should investigate. Archery lessons are necessary if you want to go bow hunting.

MAKING A STOVE

Cooking in the wild is a little different from cooking in a kitchen with stoves, ovens, and microwaves, but it can be even more rewarding and delicious.

Grill and griddle

If you find yourself without a surface to cook on, you can always use temporary grills like a piece of chain-link fence or even chicken wire. Keep in mind that many of these metals are galvanized and will release zinc into your foods and the air when heated—this is not good for your health and should only be done if you have no alternatives. Alternatively, you can use thin and flat pieces of rock, like slate, or ceramic tiles as a griddle or skillet. (You can also use sheets of metal, but the same risks of galvanized metal apply.) The best way to do this is to set up a support frame above the ground and place your grill or griddle on top. Start a fire next to this structure, wait for some coal to form, and brush the coals underneath the grill.

Spit

A spit is a traditional way of cooking many types of animals. All you need is to skewer the carcass with a stick that can be suspended over a fire. Make sure to keep rotating the spit occasionally to ensure it cooks evenly.

Earth oven

An earth oven is a valuable way of cooking that requires very few innovative materials. You just need to dig a hole big enough for your food to fit in—a depth of about six feet will work for large items. Light a fire at the bottom of the pit and let it burn out to coals. Then, cover the hot coals with some rocks; a layer of grass or vegetation for moisture; then your food. Next, you need to cover the food with more vegetation, rocks, and dirt to seal it in the hole. Depending on the type and size of your food, it can take up to 12 hours to cook, so this method is best saved for larger prey items.

Stone oven

A stone oven is a simple way to use rocks for retaining heat. You will need to create an elevated platform; back and sidewalls; and a roof out of rocks. Try to choose flatter rocks that will have fewer holes when stacked upon each other. You can also make a round oven, but make sure to leave an opening for your food to fit through. You can start a fire at the base and then place your food upon the platform just above the fire. The rocks will help to retain a higher temperature inside the oven.

SOLAR COOKING

For those times when you cannot build a fire or set up a grill for cooking food, you can always use the sun.

- **Dehydrating:** Many kinds of foods, including fruit and meat, can be dehydrated, using the sun or heat, and safely consumed. Jerky is a great example. Dehydrating works best in very hot regions where you may not be able to find enough firewood, like out in the desert. You just need to slice and lay out your foods in the sun for them to dry. This can take a long time depending on the type of food, and you will need to watch out that other animals do not steal it. You can also dry out foods next to a fire. This works well for fruits that you may not want to cook but still need to preserve.

- **Solar oven:** You can use the sun's rays to cook foods using some carefully placed reflectors. Solar ovens are sold in camping and survivalist stores but can also be made at home. You simply need to create a box or grill (cardboard, plastic, or metal can work) with a mirror or similarly reflective surfaces like aluminum foil or shiny metals. The reflectors can be attached to one side or on all four sides like flaps. You can also buy solar ovens shaped like satellite dishes. Most models also use a clear layer of plastic to cover the food and retain heat inside the box. Once you have aligned the oven correctly, the mirrors will reflect the sun's rays directly into the box and onto your food. Solar ovens can become extremely hot and can cook all kinds of food and disinfect water by boiling.

PREPAREDNESS AND SAFETY

Being prepared can make the difference between survival and starvation. While you are out in the wilderness, you must use your time wisely. Many of these cooking methods require a lot of grunt work— you need to collect firewood, tinder, and kindling; find a suitable location; transport your food and water; dig holes; carve sticks; stack rocks; etc. You need to do all of these tasks before you can even begin cooking. It is best to do this before you begin fatiguing from hunger. If you are prepared today, you are investing in your survival tomorrow.

You may not have access to firewood and be forced to rely on the heat of the sun. You may find yourself in a very damp environment where your tinder refuses to ignite. You may struggle to find palatable prey—forced to eat frogs and insects. You cannot let any of these obstacles stand in the way of your survival.

It is also important to remain aware of your surroundings and be careful when cooking food in a survival situation. The odors of cooking food can attract predators of all sizes, from the small and opportunistic scavengers that steal from right beneath your nose to the larger ones that could easily make a meal of you!

There is also no burn unit out in the wild. Never take chances playing with fire and hot objects. Always use long sticks to push coals around; never handle hot food with your bare hands; triple-check that your fires and pokers are completely extinguished when you are finished; and, if possible, have a supply of water nearby for emergencies.

WATER

In my previous book, *Practical Survival Skills: First Aid & Natural Medicines You Need to Know to Keep You Healthy & Fit In a Survival Situation*, I discuss finding water out in the wild to cure dehydration. I need to reiterate the importance of never drinking water straight from the source—no matter how thirsty you may be. Untreated water will kill you much faster than dehydration. It may be filled with chemical contaminants, parasites, pathogens, and dangerous waste products. You need to know how to make water safe for drinking, but you also need to know where to find it.

Drinking "water alternatives" is never a good idea, and even in desperate situations, you should avoid drinking urine, blood, alcohol, or seawater (including sea ice). These are not realistic alternatives—they will exacerbate the dehydration, poison your body with toxic substances that it has already worked to remove, and can lead to the transmission of viruses and diseases.

Where to Find Water

Desert habitats:

- One of the best tips for finding water in the desert is to watch other animals. Birds and most mammals will lead you to water if you can follow them. Look out for tracks and other signs.

- Collect dew and condensation: Metal objects work especially well, but if you have a tent, use it, too. Set up your objects at night and collect dew before dawn. Use a piece of fabric to wipe the moisture up.
- Look for groundwater: Look for any patches of vegetation and dig a well. It is best to do this at the lowest elevations possible, so don't waste your time digging at the top of a dune. Several deserts have massive rivers flowing below the surface.
- Rock crevices: Check deep within these areas for even the slightest bit of moisture and use a piece of fabric to wipe it up.
- Check your surroundings: Look at the landscape in which you find yourself and identify high and low points. Look for areas where water would naturally collect.
- Collect transpiration from the vegetation by wrapping them in plastic bags. The plants will collect moisture through their roots and emit it via the leaves which can be collected.

Forests:

- Most types of forests will have lakes, rivers, streams, and creeks that are your best bet of finding drinking water.
- You can often hear running water if you listen carefully.
- Assess the landscape and identify valleys and ravines where water will naturally travel and always head downstream.

Grasslands and savannas:

- Grasslands and savannas are arid or semiarid environments where water is likely to be scarce, but you may be able to find a seasonal stream, river, or watering hole used by animals. Follow the animals, especially large herds traveling early in the morning before sunrise.
- You may be able to find dry riverbeds. Dig wells in these riverbeds to see if they release any water.
- Look for the lowest points in the landscape where water will flow.
- Investigate rock crevices.

Jungles and rainforests:

- Jungles generally receive large volumes of rainfall which you can easily collect by setting up a tent or leaves to direct the rainfall into a container.
- During certain seasons, rain may be rare. Follow the animals to see where they go to drink.
- High humidity levels will make it easier to collect water from condensation. Set up metal objects and large surfaces like the walls of a tent to collect and direct water into a container. Large leaves will also work.
- Many jungle plants can be a source of water, as they trap it in their large leaves, hollow trunks, or roots. Some plants even store water inside their stems and branches. (Be careful to avoid poisonous plants and discolored water.)

Mountains:

- Mountains are a good place to look for valleys and ravines where rivers and streams flow.
- Snowfall and glaciers near mountaintops will also provide good water for drinking.

Tundra or polar:

- Cold environments are like deserts because they usually have no liquid water: It is all locked up in ice. However, you can easily harvest this ice and melt it down. Whether you can find actual ice or permafrost, both can be melted down and purified for drinking.

Woodlands and scrubs:

- You may be able to find streams or rivers in these types of habitats.
- Woodlands, scrubs, and especially other kinds of Mediterranean habitats generally receive a lot of dew in the early mornings which can be collected by shaking it off of the vegetation.

- You can also source moisture directly from the vegetation by wrapping and sealing them in plastic bags. The plant will absorb moisture through its roots and transpire through its leaves which can be collected in the plastic bags.

Coastal habitats:

- Despite the looming presence of the ocean, you can often find safe drinking water in coastal dunes and forests by digging a well.
- You can also collect early morning dew from the vegetation and flat surfaces like tents and metal objects.

Water Stills

You can construct a water still in most environments. They are used to collect condensation from vegetation and from the ground. To build a still, you will need a large, flat, and waterproof sheet (like plastic or tent fabric); a bucket or water container; some rocks or weighted objects; a digging implement (sticks work); and preferably some vegetation.

You will need to dig a hole into the ground deep enough to fit your bucket or water container and at least a few feet wide. The hole should be tapered down toward the center. Place your water container in the center of the hole and decorate the walls with lush vegetation. Then, cover the whole with your waterproof sheet using weights around the edges to secure it and a weight in the center so that it droops down. The purpose is for condensation to form on this sheet and drip down into your water container. Sunshine will help to speed this process up. If possible, you can insert a drinking tube into the water container so that you can access the water without disturbing the setup.

Since the water collected by a still is produced through the processes of evaporation and condensation, it is usually safe to drink straight away, as it has been "distilled." However, you can always boil and filter it just to be safe.

Water Purification

At this point, you've managed to collect some water, but now, you need to purify it. No matter how clean it may look, don't risk drinking it as is. Water purification involves two main steps: boiling to kill harmful pathogens and filtering to remove toxic chemicals and sediments. Doing just one of these steps is not good enough.

Boiling

Water collected from the environment should be boiled for at least 10 minutes to ensure that you kill all viruses, bacteria, and parasites.

Sand Filtration

Using a few materials, you can easily construct your own water filter. You need some type of water container to fill up from the top and drain from the bottom.

You will also need an assortment of filtration materials which can depend on what you have at hand: small rocks/pebbles, gravel, coarse sand/fine sand, charcoal, grasses, cotton wool, or fabric. It is best to thoroughly boil each of these materials before using them in your filter to ensure they are as clean and sterile as possible.

You will assemble the filter by placing the finest material layer at the base and assembling coarser materials in each successive layer. Try to ensure each layer is ideally one-inch thick. These are just suggestions, and you will have to work with the materials that are available to you in your environment:

- The first layer should be something like cotton wool or a wadded ball of fabric.
- Then, add a layer of charcoal which you can produce with some fire—you can separate this into two layers—dust, and small, crushed pieces.
- Now, add some layers of dry grass.
- Next, a layer of very fine sand
- Then a layer of coarse sand
- Then a layer of gravel
- Followed by a layer of small pebbles
- Top with some larger pebbles.
- If possible, secure the top of the filter with another layer of fabric to catch any large pieces of debris from entering the filter in the first place.
- Suspend your filter so that you can pour water at the top and collect it at the bottom. The

longer the water takes to filter through, the better!

- Look for any impurities before you drink it to make sure the filter is working correctly. If the water is still discolored or smells bad, you may need to redesign your setup and add more layers.
- If you do not have access to a suitable container, you can also use the setup where you have successive layers of fabric to contain the filtration materials.

Solar Distillation

Similar to the water still mentioned previously, you can use evaporation and condensation to make water drinkable. When water evaporates, it leaves behind all chemicals and pathogens, condensing as pure water.

You will need to follow a similar procedure beginning by digging a hole. This method works best with two containers: one with the water needing to be filtered and another to collect the condensation. You can place both containers into your hole and cover it with a waterproof sheet. Make sure the edges of the sheet are secure by packing sand and rocks around the perimeter. Then, place a weight right above your clean collection container to direct the droplets.

Over a day or two, the sun will shine down on your solar still and cause the untreated water to evaporate. It will condense on the sheet and drip down into your collection container where you will be able to drink it.

Filtration Straws

These devices are sold in camping and survival stores. They are thick, tube-like straws that you can use to drink directly from untreated water out in the environment. Inside the tubes are sophisticated filtration systems similar to the sand filters, but they often contain special disinfectants and microfilters that can ensure all heavy metals, toxins, and bacteria will be removed. Filtration straws have a limited life span but are usually quite affordable and are small and easy to carry around. They are an excellent investment for anyone that enjoys venturing out into the wild. LifeStraw, Sawyer, and Membrane Solutions produce reputable filtration straws.

Stone Boiling

One of the significant limitations of boiling water in a survival situation is that you may not have a heat-proof container that you can safely place over a fire. In this case, you can use the hot rock method. Heat some clean, smooth rocks in a fire and then transfer them into whatever container your water is stored in. This could be a piece of vegetation or animal skin. Keep replacing the rocks as they transfer their heat to the water, and eventually, it will come to a boil. Make sure it boils for at least 10 minutes.

T-Shirt and Fabric Filtration

Fabric and clothing make a helpful addition to a sand filter but are a last resort when used by themselves. Clothing can be used to remove some of the sediments found in water, making it clearer and less cloudy. However, this will not help to remove microscopic pathogens, heavy metals, or other environmental pollutants.

5

UNCONVENTIONAL FOOD SOURCES

You may be asking, "Why do I need to go through all this effort—collecting firewood, building an oven, making utensils—just so I can enjoy some berries, nuts, and seeds out in the woods?" Well, plant foods are certainly important, but they will not sustain you—not for very long, anyway. Now, we have reached the part where we talk about alternative and unconventional sources of food—insects, bugs, and other small, crunchy creatures.

The thought of eating insects is usually met with understandable trepidation, but this does not do them justice. People have eaten—and relied—on insect protein for thousands of years. Many cultures around the world still consume them, from deep-fried scorpions, to flour made from mealworms, to barbequed mopani worms wrapped in bacon. Bugs are not really that different from the seafood delicacies like lobsters, crayfish, crab, shrimp, or prawns. In fact, most of the insects on land eat a far cleaner and more vegetarian diet. They are also found in abundance in most habitats, they are incredibly easy to collect, and simple to prepare.

NUTRITIONAL VALUE

There are over 900 thousand different species of insects on Earth—that's not including other types of creepy crawlies like arachnids, millipedes, and centipedes. About 1,900 are considered edible—being digestible, nonpoisonous, and found in reasonable abundance. You also get different kinds of edible worms and mollusks, including snails. Naturally, the nutritional value will be just as diverse. It is also important to remember that most insects undergo several different stages in their life cycle, including larvae, pupae, eggs, and adults—some of which can offer more nutrition and calories than others.

In general though, insect proteins are comparable to traditional "meat." They meet our requirements for amino acids; monounsaturated and polyunsaturated fats; antioxidants, vitamins such as A, B2, B5, B7, B9, C, D, E, and K; and minerals including copper, iron, magnesium, manganese, phosphorus, selenium, and zinc. Table 1 shows some of the macronutrient breakdowns of traditional proteins compared to some insect proteins. You can see that crickets offer more protein per calories than beef, salmon, or even tofu. Insects have a reasonable amount of fat, though some are quite high in saturated fat. Insects also, uniquely, offer fiber in the form of chitin from their exoskeletons, unlike any other kind of mammalian or avian meat.

Nutritional content in 200 calories of:	Protein (g)	Fat (g)	Saturated Fat (g)	Fiber (%)
Lean Beef	22.4	11.2	4.4	0
Salmon	20.4	13.4	3.0	0
Crickets	**31.0**	*8.1*	2.6	**7.2**
Mealworms	*16.2*	14.8	**4.9**	2.5
Eggs	19.2	**15.2**	4.8	0
Tofu	24.6	12.6	2.7	2.7

It is also easier to identify poisonous bugs than it is to identify poisonous plants. Most poisonous bugs proudly display their toxic qualities using bright coloration and aggressive defenses, whereas plants can be tricky and sly.

NATURE'S LARDER

Everything that we could possibly need, nature has in store. Think back to the many different survival shows that have aired on TV—how the contestants scrambled to collect as many coconuts as they could, spent hours in the baking sun trying to catch fish, and slashed their feet open while attempting to hunt wild boar in forests —all the while, fistfuls of crickets sat peacefully in the trees singing them to sleep each evening. These people completely ignore a zero-effort food source right in front of them.

Insects You Can Eat

Generally Safe

1. Grasshoppers, crickets, locusts, and katydids

These insects can be found at the top of most edible insects lists because they have so much to offer. They are found pretty much everywhere, they are easy to locate, and they are easy to catch—all you need is a net. They can be eaten whole but can also be "winnowed" like grains to remove their legs and antennae; they are also easy to cook, requiring only a few minutes of roasting over a fire. Of course, you can also dry and grind them down to make cricket flour as well. They seem to have a mild, nutty flavor.

2. Ants and termites

These small insects are perhaps the most abundant in the world. You can collect ants using a sugary bait or simply poke a nest with a stick. You should definitely raid one of their nests to reveal thousands of adults but also the pupa and larva—plump and juicy for the taking. The easiest way to prepare them is to drop them in some water while collecting, and when you have a good amount, boil them. You can eat them raw but run the risk of getting bitten or stung.

3. Grubs

Grubs are the large, squirming, worm-like larva of beetles, though the term can also refer to any kind of insect larva. Depending on the species, they can be as large as a finger. You can find grubs in leaf litter and underneath moist, rotting logs. They are rich in fat that can help sustain you for a long time. Roast grubs by skewering them onto a stick and cooking them over a fire.

4. Earthworms

Easy to identify and common in moist soils, earthworms make a good and slimy nutritional supplement to a forager's diet. Though they can be eaten raw, they are also subject to parasites and usually have guts full of grainy sand. You can make them safer and more palatable by boiling them first, though there is not much in the way of flavor.

5. Wood lice

These are not actually insects but crustaceans—more closely related to lobsters and crabs than beetles. You can find them underneath rocks, rotting logs, and moist leaf litter, and they can be quite easy to catch in decent amounts. They need to be cooked thoroughly, so boil them first to kill internal parasites; then, you can try roasting or frying them for some texture.

6. Beetles

Beetles can be found in all different shapes and sizes, and many are safe to eat once cooked. Most of the Western world is already consuming a type of beetle—cochineal beetles—used to make several red food dyes.

You will need to avoid brightly colored species, especially red and yellow kinds, but most brown and green beetles are good. You can remove their legs before boiling, roasting, or frying them. You can eat their exoskeletons or choose just the meat inside.

7. Caterpillars

Caterpillars are like little sausages of the insect world. They are soft-bodied, slow moving, and full of nutrition. However, most of them can be quite dangerous and should only be a last resort. Avoid any caterpillar with spines; hairy or any spiny protrusions; and stick to bland colors. Try to stick to caterpillars that resemble silkworms. You can skewer them and cook them over a fire or boil them to kill all the internal parasites before eating.

Notable Mentions

1. Spiders

Though almost all spiders are edible and nonpoisonous, many are venomous and treacherous to catch and handle. Tarantulas are eaten as a delicacy in many countries. They are covered in fine, irritating hairs which must first be burned off. They can also give you a nasty bite which can cause nausea, fevers, and infection. You can eat them if you have no other options but take caution.

2. Scorpions

The general rule for scorpions is this: If they have a large stinger and small claws, they are highly venomous, but if they have a small stinger and large claws, they are less dangerous. All scorpions, however, are venomous and can sting. Larger scorpion stings can kill people, while smaller scorpions may feel like a bee sting. However, they are quite tasty when roasted over a fire, so if you are brave enough to try and catch one, they will be worth your while. Simply cut the stinger off completely to be safe.

3. Camel spiders

These feisty little creatures look like a cross between a scorpion and a spider. They are also called sun spiders and look as if they have five pairs of legs due to their enlarged set of palps at the front of their bodies. They are extremely tenacious and hunt down their prey by chasing them. They grow to decent sizes, making them a reasonable option for eating. They are not venomous but can and will bite.

4. Bees and wasps

Try to avoid eating bees and wasps, that is, if you can manage to catch them in the first place! It is not worth the effort of getting stung or attacked by a hive. If you manage to find a beehive, you are much better off trying to harvest the honey than the bees themselves. You can try to smoke them out using smoldering vegetation if it becomes absolutely necessary, but I certainly do not suggest it.

Unnoted Mentions

5. Flies and maggots

Sure, you can often find flies and maggots in abundance around rotting foods and carcasses, but these insects are riddled with pathogens including *E. coli* and cholera. Do not eat them. Even when cooked, they will be covered in toxic chemicals and waste products.

6. Cockroaches

Roaches are definitely more sanitary than flies, and most varieties are actually edible. You can treat them in the same way as beetles, making sure to cook them thoroughly. However, roaches can be extremely difficult to catch, and you will probably use more energy in your attempts than you will get out in calories. Several species are famous for feeding on trash and waste, and you would want to avoid these. However, most of them are vegetarian or detritivores, feeding on leaf litter.

Bug	Where to Look For Them	Season and Activity Period
Grasshoppers	Grassy areas	All year round; daytime
Crickets	Grassy areas	All year round; nighttime
Locusts	Many habitats	After drought; daytime
Katydids	Mostly in trees	Summer; daytime and nighttime
Ants	Many habitats	All year round; daytime
Grubs	In moist soils, under leaf litter, and in rotting logs	Summer; daytime and nighttime
Earthworms	In moist soils	Spring; daytime
Wood Lice	In rotting logs and leaf litter	Fall, winter, and spring; nighttime
Beetles	Many habitats	Summer; daytime
Caterpillars	Leafy vegetation	Spring; daytime
Spiders	Many habitats, under rocks or vegetation	Summer; daytime and nighttime
Scorpions	Arid habitats	All year round but mainly summer; nighttime
Camel Spiders	Arid habitats	Summer; nighttime
Bees	Many habitats	Spring and summer; daytime
Wasps	Many habitats	Spring and summer; daytime
Flies and Maggots	Near rotting food and carrion in many habitats	All year round but most abundant in summer; daytime
Cockroaches	Many habitats; under leaf litter	Spring, summer, and fall; nighttime

SAFETY TIPS

- Always cook your food thoroughly.
- Avoid aggressive bugs that bite and sting or those with defenses like spines or hairs.
- Avoid most caterpillars: They can also eat poisonous plants which begin to accumulate in

their bodies.

- Avoid most strong-smelling bugs which can contain pungent poisons. (However, most stink bugs, ironically, are safe to eat.)
- Avoid snails and slugs if you can: They carry several parasites and often eat poisonous plants that accumulate in their bodies.
- If you are unsure about whether or not an insect or bug is safe to eat, carry out the universal edibility test.
- If you eat bugs with stingers, cut the stingers off at the base before handling and cooking them. Even a dead scorpion can sting you.
- Stay away from bright and high contrast colors —especially red, yellow and black.
- Stay away from urban bugs that have very likely been exposed to pesticides.

CATCHING BUGS

Pitfall Trap

A pitfall trap is a common feature among bug enthusiasts that can also catch other small prey. A pitfall trap is just a hole in the ground. You should try to make the walls of the hole smooth or place a bucket inside to prevent insects from crawling back up once they fall in. You can also make the sides of the hole tapered with a narrower opening, and it should be deep enough so that jumping creatures cannot escape.

You should place a few pitfall traps in different types of habitats to increase your chances of success. Look for places where you can see insect activity, and place one in a moist area under tree cover, another in an open or grassy area, one close to a waterway, one near a rocky outcrop, etc. You can choose to include some bait inside the bucket as well—the most common type is some rotting fruit which can be used to attract beetles. You must also be aware of the different activity periods: Some insects are active in the day while others are active at night. You need to check the traps at different times of the day: from dawn, to midday, to dusk.

The pitfall trap will need to be protected so that other animals do not steal your insects. To do this, you can create a roof that sits an inch or two above the opening of the hole. Use rocks as pillars to hold the roof up, and leave enough gaps for insects to pass through and fall into the hole. The roof can also help protect other animals that may be unlucky enough to fall into your trap, like mice or frogs.

Nets

Nets are another simple way to catch insects like grasshoppers. You can construct a simple net out of many types of materials including clothing, sleeping bags, or tents. Run the net over a grassy area a few times, and you are bound to catch some insects.

Light Traps

Light traps are also effective for catching several nocturnal insects or those that navigate using the sun or moon. This can include cicadas, several types of moths, and even beetles. A light trap requires a large, preferably white sheet and a light source. Hang a sheet up vertically with as much surface area as possible, then set up the light source behind the sheet so that it is illuminated. During the night, this light source will attract several thousands of insects which you can easily scoop into a container. They will be gone by dawn though, so you must collect them during the night. If you are using fire as a light source, practice your fire safety tips and make sure the sheet cannot catch fire.

COOKING BUGS

While most insects and bugs are technically edible when raw, they can be quite unpalatable and often carry several types of parasites which can make you sick further down the line. However, they can become quite delectable if you can cook them properly:

- Try to remove the legs, antennae, wings, and other appendages before you cook and eat different kinds of bugs. These can be hard to chew and offer little nutritional value.
- You need to either boil them for a few minutes or cook them in a high heat—this can include

roasting or frying. Eating insects and bugs raw is not recommended.

- You can make protein-rich powder from most types of bugs. Simply roast them until they are completely dehydrated and then grind them up into a fine powder.
- Do not forget some seasoning—as with any food, they taste much better with salt and pepper, some chili, lemon juice, or sautéed in butter.
- For smaller insects like ants or termites, you can sprinkle them over other dishes or wrap a bunch of them up in an edible leaf and roast them over a fire to make them more satiating.

6

THE HUNTER-GATHERER

"We are a part of nature, not apart from it."

— MARC BEKOFF

Hunting tends to draw a lot of allure and prestige. However, when you find yourself in a dire survival situation, where your life is on the line, relying on a successful hunt can often be a foolish and futile mistake. There are no guarantees when you hunt for food. For our ancestors, going on a hunt was no small task. It often involved weeks of tracking and scouting to identify the ideal prey, their location, and their movements. Hunts could only be carried out during certain seasons when herds were migrating or reproducing.

I can speak from my own experiences—spending several hours out in the wilderness where I collected materials and constructed a sophisticated trap. I managed to get it all set up and sat down to wait, in eager anticipation, for an unlucky prey animal to stray across my path. I must have spent half the day crouched down behind a bush trying to be as silent as possible.

Finally, a suitable prey animal entered my line of sight, and I watched with bated breath as it meandered into my trap. Everything went exactly as I had hoped, and the trap was released, capturing the animal. But when the time came for me to retrieve my dinner… the sight of me must have given it a sudden burst of adrenaline— enough to break free and run away back into the cover. I had a very sad meal of defeat that evening.

I was sure that I would be able to catch an animal, so I spent no time collecting other sources of food—I was low on water, and I didn't even have enough firewood to last the night. This is one of the major downsides of trying to rely on medium or large prey to survive—they want to live, and they will fight with tooth and nail to escape. Your chances of success are astronomically low. Take a look at how successful some wild predators are in their hunts: Lions are only successful about 20% of the time; wolves and polar bears even less so; and tigers have a measly success rate of about 7.5% (Fair, 2020).

My point here is not to dismay you completely—only to emphasize the fact that hunting takes a lot of time and energy which are your two most crucial resources when you are in the wilderness. You should always try to make sure you are stocked up on other essentials like berries, nuts, seeds, insects, water, and firewood before you go out trying to catch prey animals. These plant foods will help to sustain you while you are hunting, and they will be a valuable fallback if your attempts should fail.

LOCATING ANIMALS

Now that your hopes and dreams of taking down a moose with your bare hands have been dashed, let's look at some of the ways you can actually increase your chances of success while hunting.

When you are out in the wild, the most practical and accessible types of prey animals are going to be the small ones: rodents, rabbits, birds, fish, reptiles, amphibians, and the bugs and insects mentioned previously. You should spend a good amount of time observing the animals by trying to understand their patterns and behaviors, where they feed, where they sleep, where they drink, and where they socialize.

Signs of Animal Activity

There are several signs that you can look out for out in the wild that indicate the activity of different animals:

Footprints: An animal's footprints can provide a lot of information. You can figure out what kind of animal it is, how big they are, whether they are moving alone or in a group, which direction they are traveling in, and how fast they are moving. Though this skill can take some time to develop, it is also intuitive and simple to figure out. You should try to learn how to identify the footprints of different groups of animals so that you don't waste your time and effort tracking animals that would be undesirable to try and hunt:

- Cat footprints have four toe pads and one large pad in the middle. They are usually quite round and have no claw marks because the animals hold their claws in the retracted position when walking. Cats come in many different sizes, and their prints reflect this, with house cat prints being very small compared to that of a cougar, for example. Cats walk by placing their hind feet into the print made by the front feet, forming a single track.

- Canine footprints are similar to cat prints, but they will have distinct claw marks. They can also range in size. Canines do not walk in the same way as cats. Instead, their hind feet will usually produce their own set of prints. Foxes are an exception, with a similar gait to that of felines.

- Animals from the weasel family will produce footprints showing five toes, each with a claw mark. They are usually very small compared to dog or cat prints and leave a pungent smell behind due to the animal's scent glands. Animals in the weasel family include weasels, martens, badgers, otters, skunks, minks, wolverines, and ferrets.

- Bears, raccoons, and opossums can be identified by their footprints because the front feet are different to the back feet. Their back feet are usually more elongated, like a human, whereas the front feet are rounder. They will produce a print with five toes and claw marks on each. Raccoons often have long fingers which are visible in their prints, bears will have distinctively large prints, and opossums have opposable thumbs which are visible in the prints of their front feet.

- Animals in the rodent family include rabbits, hares, mice, rats, squirrels, gophers, chipmunks, porcupines, hedgehogs, and beavers. Their front feet are different to their back feet with four toes on the front and five on the back. Their back feet are slightly elongated with a noticeable heel portion and usually have visible claw marks. Hares and rabbits have back feet that are much longer than their front feet and will form prints in side-by-side pairs rather than alternating due to their jumping gait.

- Hoofed animals include even-toed and odd-toed groups. The only odd-toed animals in North America and Europe will be horses and donkeys which are easily identified by their round hooves that have triangular wedges at the back. Even-toed animals include deer, antelope, pigs, boars, cattle, sheep, goats, and camels. Skilled trackers can easily identify deer species from their prints, but this skill can take several years to master. The main takeaways for you are to be able to identify the direction in which the animals are traveling. Most of these even-toed animals will have a pair of teardrop-shaped hooves with two small heel marks. Elk, cows, and bighorn sheep have relatively simple teardrop shapes, whereas deer have more complicated shapes. All will have the pointed end of the teardrop in the front of their foot and the rounded part at the back next to the small heel marks.

- Birds generally have three forward-pointing toes and one backward-pointing toe on their feet. Owls differ in having one of the forward-pointing toes angled out more to the side and sometimes backward. Some useful features to look out for are the size of the prints and whether they are solitary or in a group. Waterbirds will have webbing in between the toes, and predatory birds will have large talon marks.

- Reptiles have feet with five toes—one of which is usually much longer than the rest. They have splayed, simple footprints, and you can often see where their bellies lay or were dragged while walking. Reptiles can also gallop at high speeds which will leave marks where their front and back legs fall more in line with each other. Snakes make markings on the ground that are quite distinctive but can be overlooked. They will push sand and debris to the sides as they slither, leaving a shallow mark where they drag themselves.

- Amphibians have footprints with five toes, each tipped with a large round pad. Their markings will show up well on the muddy banks, or rivers, lakes, and streams. Since they jump, the back feet will usually be found next to each other.

Animal trails: Regular animal traffic will lead to well-worn paths and trails, often following the most desirable routes to and from feeding, drinking, and resting sites. You will be able to see footprints and droppings along these trails to confirm whether they are currently being used or not. Animals will use different routes during different times of the year, and some paths may be abandoned.

Rubs: Several types of animals will rub against the bases of trees to scratch itches, mark their scent, and to display dominance. You should keep an eye out for trees that are damaged in this way, revealing their pale inner bark. You can tell if the trees have been recently visited by whether or not there is a noticeable scent and by the dryness or wetness of the inner bark. Trees will heal over time if left alone, leaving behind a scar where the animals damaged it. You may also be able to find broken pieces of antler or fur at these sites.

Dust baths: Several species of birds partake in dust baths each day. You can identify them by the presence of fine dust or sand and several footprints and feathers. The dust will be highly disturbed.

Fur and feathers: While scouting a potential animal trail, look out for any pieces of hair or fur that may get stuck on the vegetation. Thorny and brambly plants will grab onto animal fur and help you to determine what kind of animals may be using the trail.

Gnawing and chewing marks: Look for markings on trees, branches, twigs, leaves, grasses, nuts, and even bones. Browsing animals will nibble on a few leaves of a tree before moving on to the next tree. Grazing animals will either chew off the tops of grasses or rip them from their roots. Several types of rodents, especially porcupines, will gnaw on dry wood and dry bones to help keep their teeth healthy. All of these signs can indicate the presence and activity of different animals.

Droppings: Animals can be identified by their droppings. Deer will produce smooth and round pellets made of fine grassy material. Rodents will produce smaller, more elongated pellets, while rabbits and hares tend to produce more spherical pellets. Antelope, goats, and sheep also produce pellets, but they are usually not smooth and contain larger pieces of undigested grass. Beaver droppings will be rich in woody material. Carnivorous animals do not generally produce pellets, and their droppings will be more pungent, containing undigested animal material like fur, bones, and claws. Animals like otters that eat mainly mollusks will have pieces of shell in their droppings. You will need to look at the size, shape, and type of materials in the droppings to identify what kind of animal it came from. Bird droppings also range in color, size, shape, and consistency. Predatory birds can often produce pellets with small pieces of undigested animal parts like bones, feathers, and fur. Insectivore birds will have droppings that contain the exoskeletons of their prey.

Types of Animals

Birds

It is crucial to be as quiet as possible when scouting for birds, and you also need to be patient. Some of the best places to find birds will be near water sources where they are forced to land. Whether they are solitary or gregarious birds, they will come to drink early in the morning and often throughout the day as well. Most birds are diurnal, meaning they are active during the day and don't see well at night. You can use this to your advantage by trying to catch them at dusk when they go for their last drink of the evening. Exploit their roosting spots where they go to sleep each night. Nesting season is a particularly good time to try and catch birds, as many species will not leave their eggs even if they are approached by predators. Their eggs are another good food source you should make use of as well. You can catch birds using nets, either by targeting them in their nests or observing flight patterns—they will choose similar routes through obstacles like trees and crevices which you can exploit. All kinds of birds are edible and safe to eat once cooked properly, but be wary of handling the raw meat: Make sure to wash before and after to avoid the risk of *Salmonella* infection.

Small Mammals

Animals like rabbits, hairs, small antelope, or deer can generally be found in greater abundance than larger prey. They are also easier to transport, butcher, and cook. You will need to identify what kind of prey you would like to try and catch, and then, determine where and when they feed. It is useful to be able to identify the tracks and signs of these animals. For example, rabbits and hares may use the same pathways through dense shrubs and grasses, leaving a small highway bare of leaves and debris. Dawn and dusk are usually the best times to try and hunt for small mammals; they are early risers that like to get their day started before the heat of the sun bears down on them. All mammals are edible; however, some mammals can be particularly voracious and will defend themselves against attack. Try to avoid getting bitten or scratched, which could result in a rabies infection. The livers of most apex predators should be avoided, however, due to their toxic levels of vitamin A.

Reptiles

Most reptiles can be eaten; however, they can be particularly difficult to catch. You should look for lizards, geckos, snakes, turtles, and larger reptiles like caimans, alligators, and crocodiles. The best time to find them is when they are basking in the sun, usually on rocks. They will be particularly sluggish at dawn. Obviously, you will need to be wary of their dangers—many snakes are venomous, and large reptiles can easily make a meal out of you if you are not careful. Reptiles are also a common source of *Salmonella* infection, and care must be taken to ensure you do not eat them raw if possible; wash your hands thoroughly when you are done handling the meat. Reptiles can be cooked and treated similarly to most birds and will taste best when roasted over a fire, allowing them to brown slightly.

Amphibians

Frogs, toads, and salamanders can make easy prey. However, you should try to avoid toads because many of them are poisonous. You can tell them apart because toads tend to have drier skin and live in drier habitats, whereas frogs will have moist skin and can always be found near water. You should also avoid any species that have bright coloration or flashy patterns on their skin, as this is also a good indicator that they are poisonous. Most amphibians are nocturnal. You can locate frogs by listening for their croaks in wetlands, swampy areas, and near other types of water sources. You can usually catch them with your hands if you are quick enough, but nets work great, too. Salamanders are slightly rarer though you can spot them swimming in shallow waters if you have a torch. Amphibians are generally skinned before eating, though if you roast them over a fire, their skin is thin enough to burn away. They are a good source of protein.

Fish

Freshwater and marine fish are all great sources of fat and protein. You can try and catch them using makeshift fishing hooks made from any sharp materials and string or sinew; however, other types of traps would probably work better. You should try looking for fish in clear waters where they are protected from strong currents, especially under the cover of foliage. Almost all freshwater fish are safe to eat, but some can be dangerous. Large catfish or sturgeon would not make easy prey, for example, and their spines can easily cause wounds. There are several poisonous marine fish, but you can usually identify them because they have long, sharp, and showy spines. All fish contain parasites and worms, but marine fish are usually safer and can often be eaten raw. However, you should cook them just to be safe and make them more palatable.

Crustaceans

Crabs, shrimp, lobsters, crayfish, and other types of shellfish can be found in freshwater and marine environments. Most of them are nocturnal, but some crabs are active during the day. You can usually spot them because they make small breathing holes in the sand. They will often be attracted by meaty bait. A simple way to trap them is to use a container with a small, tapered opening that is easy to get into but difficult to get out of. These can be made with woven grass or plastic waste. You can also catch many types of species with your hands if you dig in the right places—just be careful of nipping pincers. Small shrimp will be found near algal mats on which they feed. You should cook all crustaceans and prepare them by removing the legs, antennae, and gutting them first.

Mollusks

There are many kinds of mollusks that make for good eating, including clams, mussels, snails, barnacles, squid, and octopi. In freshwater environments, snails and mussels will be the most common, and they are very easy to catch, being slow or completely sessile. Marine species can be found on beaches and in rock pools. Mussels, clams, oysters, and barnacles will stick to rocks and need to be pried off with a knife, while octopi often become trapped in tidal pools and are simple to catch by hand or net. Keep in mind that octopi have sharp beaks that can bite, and their suckers can also be painful. You can also find marine snails on the beach by looking for their air bubbles when the waves move out, though they are also attracted to meat and can be baited. Most marine mollusks can be eaten raw, but some cooking is recommended. Animals with closed shells can be steamed, boiled, or roasted, and the rule is to discard any that do not open once cooked, as they are probably already dead and may carry bacteria. Octopi and squid are best when scored and roasted or fried.

Starfish and Urchins

These animals can provide a good amount of vitamins and minerals but not too much in the way of calories. The best place to find them is in rock pools on the beach. You may need to pry them off of the rocks using a knife or a stick. Most starfish and other kinds of sea stars can be safely eaten after cooking them. Sea urchins can be eaten raw but are also best cooked. You just need to turn them upside down to reveal the mouth where you can insert a knife to crack them open.

TRAPS

Trapping small game is much easier than hunting. Several trap designs can be used to catch different types of animals; you just need to know where to place them. It is best to set up traps where you can see signs of animal traffic.

- **Snare:** This is a simple trap that only requires a piece of string or rope. Make a loop and secure it using a knot that can slide up and down, like a noose. Set the loop in an animal pathway or front of a den, and secure the other end to a strong branch or rock. When an animal enters the snare, the slipknot will draw tight around its body. It is critical to check your snares often, as any caught animals will quickly attract the attention of other predators.

- **Spring snare:** Snares can also be set up with trigger mechanisms that will activate when an animal becomes trapped. You can use a supple sapling to hoist your snare up into the air, effectively hanging the prey animal and killing it quickly. You will need a snare, some pieces of wood, another long piece of rope, and a springy piece of vegetation to attach it to. There are several types of triggers, though the wedge and the Y-styles are among the simplest. A wedge-style trigger uses two smooth branches. Cut a wedge out of the side from one of the branches, and then, carve a hook from the other branch so that it can fit inside the wedge. Similarly, a Y-shaped trigger uses two Y-shaped branches. They will be set up in a way that the tip of the Y-shapes hooks onto each other. Attach the snare itself to the branch with the hook and a young sapling. Bend over the sapling and secure it in place by setting the hooked branch into the wedged branch. When an animal runs through the snare, it will become trapped, setting off the trigger which will then launch it into the air.
- A deadfall trap is suitable for small prey that can be crushed with a rock, including rodents

and reptiles. A deadfall trap uses a large, heavy rock propped up by a stick, a trigger string, and bait. The purpose is to attract a prey animal to the bait placed underneath the rock. A long trigger string must be attached to the stick so that you can pull on it, causing the rock to fall. Place bait underneath the rock and wait in a hidden area for prey to approach. When they are beneath the rock, pull the trigger string, and hopefully, you can crush the prey animal. You can also avoid crushing the animals by using a box, but this can make it easier for them to escape unless you add weight to the top of the box.

- **Bird box trap:** This type of trap is almost identical to a deadfall trap, but instead of using a heavy weight to crush your prey animal, you will use a simple hollow box or cage instead. When triggered, the box will fall on the prey animal, entrapping it. It should not kill the animal. This is useful for catching fowl birds, and you can use seeds or fruit as bait inside.
- **Funnel fish trap:** You can make this type of trap using any kind of funnel-shaped object. You can use woven baskets, reeds, twigs, and branches, or a plastic bottle. You will need to build a cage-like structure in the shape of a

funnel, and this will be contained inside a larger container to entrap fish. If you use a plastic bottle, you need to cut off the conical end, flip it around, and insert it into the base end. With traps made from plant materials, there will be gaps between the branches or reeds. The size of these gaps must be small enough so that your prey of choice cannot escape through them. Place the fish trap in a location where you have seen fish swimming, and orientate it with the current and fish movements. The fish will be able to enter easily but will not be able to escape. You can catch fish and crustaceans with this type of trap—especially if you place a small amount of bait inside.

TIPS AND TRICKS

- Choose animals that can be found in abundance.
- Leave your taste preferences at home. When you've been without a decent meal for a few days, a roasted raccoon will be just as satisfying as roast beef. Take what you can get.
- When stalking prey, take your time. It is essential that you be patient and go slowly. This

will help you to remain as silent as possible and listen carefully to your surroundings.

- Use the landscape to your advantage—use tree lines, rocks, hills, and vegetation to your advantage. You need to think like a predator— remaining out of the line of sight.

- Stay downwind. Humans have a terrible sense of smell compared to other animals—which can often smell you coming long before they see or hear you.
- Birds will often ruin your hunts on purpose. They will see you from their perches and make alarm calls. All animals in the vicinity will have learned this alarm call and flee in response. If you notice birds like crows, cuckoos, or other more intelligent species watching you, it's best to try and find another area to stalk prey.

- Be opportunistic: Along with leaving taste preferences behind, you may sometimes be met with foods that you cannot eat but can be used to bait other animals. Carcasses should be exploited for their bait potential as well as for materials like sinew.
- If you use snares or other types of traps, you need to check them regularly! There is nothing more disappointing than finding a bloody mess in a snare, knowing that you managed to trap an animal but had it stolen before you could eat it.
- Make use of your weapons. If you have good aim, slinging a rock or throwing a spear can make quick work of a prey animal.

AFTER A SUCCESSFUL HUNT

If you are persistent and lucky enough to catch a prey animal of decent size, your work is not yet over. You need to be wary of your surroundings and look out for opportunistic predators. If you can carry the animal whole back to your campsite, you can do so immediately, but larger prey will need to be gutted and dressed first. You may need to walk back many miles to reach your campsite, and you should have a projectile weapon like a rock sling to deter coyotes or raccoons—not to mention larger animals like bears.

Once you begin butchering your carcass, you will also attract smaller animals like rodents and birds who will try to steal small pieces. If you have a rope, suspend your carcass in a tree while you are working on other tasks to make it as difficult as possible for animals to reach it. You can also secure meat in rivers and streams for short periods of time to hide the scent. Just ensure they are securely covered with rocks, so the current cannot wash it away. Fish will take nibbles, though, so only do this with large items.

If you are drying your food in the sun or near a fire, you need constant vigilance. You cannot afford to wander and take your eyes off. This is why smaller game often fare better in a survival situation because there will be no waste and nothing to store once you have eaten.

HOW TO BUTCHER AND COOK

Bleeding and Hanging

It is common practice to cut the throat and then hang the animal upside down by its hind legs to allow as much blood to drain as possible. This can take a few hours for larger game. It will improve the taste and make the meat more tender, as the effects of rigor mortis dissipate. You can choose to collect the blood or not. This step is not necessary, though—especially for small animals.

Skinning and Gutting

You can eat the skin of many animals—especially birds and mammals. However, some are better and easier to handle when skinned, like frogs or snakes. In some cases, you may want to cook the animal in its skin and then eat only the meat inside, such as an alligator. However, skinning is a simple process that doesn't take too much effort. You can skin the animal while it is hanging upside down or by laying them out flat on the ground. It is best to skin an animal once the body has cooled down to ambient temperature, making it easier to handle.

Begin at the center of the animal's belly and pinch some skin, pulling it upward. This will help you make a small incision. Use this incision to begin your cut all the way from the throat down to the groin. Make sure you do not pierce the muscles of the abdominal wall. You can use your fingers to separate the skin from the under-lying muscles before using a blade. Grab onto the skin and begin teasing and tearing it away from the flesh, pulling toward the sides. Again, use your fingers to break apart the connective tissues or gently slice it with a blade as you pull. This does not take too much cutting force. Pull as far to the sides as you can. For smaller animals, you may be able to pull some of the skin off the arms and legs without needing to make more cuts.

Once the abdomen and chest is exposed, you can begin to gut and remove the organs. Very carefully, make a small incision into the abdominal muscles right in the center. Great care must be taken not to pierce the intestines which lie right below these muscles. If you pierce the intestines, your meat will become tainted and inedible. Cut a line in the abdominal wall from the base of the ribs and down to the groin. You will be able to pull the muscles to either side to reveal the internal organs. Locate the stomach and the rectum. You can use a piece of string to tie these tubes off before cutting them. This will allow you to remove the entire digestive tract. (Alternatively, you can cut a circle around the anus on the outside of the body; pull the rectum and anus into the body cavity; and discard them with the rest of the digestive tract.) You should discard this away from your processing station. You will also need to remove the bladder at this stage, being careful not to pierce it or spill the contents. Both the bladder and intestines are likely to be full, so be prepared for this.

Carefully remove the liver and kidneys which you can eat after cooking. Next, you will need to open the rib cage. Depending on the size of the animal, this may be easy or quite strenuous. For smaller animals, you can simply cut through the ribs down the center of the sternum. For larger animals, you will need to cut away at the connecting tissue between the ribs and the sternum. Then, pry the rib cage open. The heart and lungs can also be eaten.

The next step is to make cuts on the inside of each limb —from the feet all the way to your central abdominal cut. Make sure to only cut skin, and don't go too deep as to cut the tendons and ligaments. Tendons and ligaments are astoundingly strong and will quickly dull your blade. The tail may also pose some challenges and should be removed. You can either cut the tail off as is or separate the bones inside so that the tail comes away with the skin.

You should now have flaps on the sides of the body that you can pull and peel off. Keep teasing and gently slicing away while you pull until the whole hide comes off. You may need to cut around the neck area, so you can also pull the facial skin off whole. You will need to finish off by cutting at the feet to remove the last few pieces of skin that are still connected.

For reptiles and amphibians with thin skin that may tear easily if you pull too hard, you can burn and singe the skin first. This will make it tougher and easier to pull off in one piece.

To gut a fish, follow a similar procedure of making an incision into the belly. Again, be careful not to pierce the guts, but once the abdomen is open, you can simply pull them out and discard them. Fish do not need to be skinned.

Butchering

In a survival situation, you do not need to worry about making aesthetically pleasing cuts. You can simply hack off a leg and roast it over a fire. However, if you do have some time, you can begin by identifying the traditional cuts of meat which are present on all quadrupedal animals

—the rump, loin, flank, etc. Cut these off the carcass by slicing with the grain of the tissues. You can also simply cut off the muscular tissue in strips. Try not to avoid the fat, as it can provide essential energy and nutrients.

Butchering a bird is a little simpler, as you can cut off the wings and legs for cooking. The breast must be separated from the keel bone. You can also butterfly a bird by spreading it out flat and cooking it without the need to butcher it prior.

Skinning other types of animals will be similar. For fish and snakes, you need to make a small incision near the head or tail and then simply pull the skin away from the muscles underneath.

Try to include fat in your cuts, as many wild animals will be very lean. You will need the fat to sustain you. Fat can also be found around the kidneys.

Defeathering

Birds will need to be defeathered, as their skin is a useful and tasty source of fat that should be consumed. You can do this either by simply burning the feathers away from the skin, or by plucking them out by hand. Boiling the carcass for a few minutes can help to loosen the feathers before you pluck them out.

Difficult Animals

Certain types of animals will be more difficult to work with than others. Examples include turtles, tortoises, porcupines, hedgehogs, etc. The shells of tortoises and turtles can be more easily removed after you boil them whole. Porcupines and hedgehogs have soft bellies that you can access to carry out the butchering, but be wary of their quills.

Cooking

We have already discussed some of the ways you can cook your wild-caught game. You can boil all types of meat, but you will need a water-tight container to do so, and it is not the tastiest method of cooking meat. You can roast pieces over a fire either using small pieces pierced with skewers or larger and more whole cuts of meat on a spit. You can grill or fry cuts of meat using a hot, flat stone or thin slab of hardwood, and you can also make use of a stone or earth oven to prepare larger pieces of meat.

Do not forget to make use of the organs and bones which contain bone marrow. You can use larger bones from the legs and ribs, cooked over a fire, and then smashed open with a rock. Organs such as the liver are a good source of vitamins and minerals, but as mentioned previously, avoid livers from predatory animals. The kidneys are also a good source of lean protein surrounded by pockets of fat. If you can crack open the braincase, the brain will also provide you with good fats.

Meat can also be preserved by drying, smoking, or salting it. You will need to cut it into thin strips and then lay them out flat to either dry in the sun or near a fire. You can create smoke by using wood chips and green foliage—ensuring it blows over the meat.

WILD EDIBLES INDEX

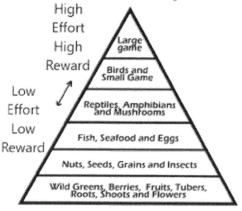

Survival Food Pyramid

High
Effort
High
Reward

Large game

Birds and Small Game

Low
Effort
Low
Reward

Reptiles, Amphibians and Mushrooms

Fish, Seafood and Eggs

Nuts, Seeds, Grains and Insects

Wild Greens, Berries, Fruits, Tubers, Roots, Shoots and Flowers

S urvival foods can be prioritized based on how easy they are to find and collect; how abundant they are; and how many nutrients and calories you can get out of them in return. The survival food pyramid is a useful tool to help you decide what to focus on foraging for when you find yourself in a survival situation.

The bulk of your diet should be composed of plant foods like berries, fruit, wild greens, shoots, flowers, roots, and tubers. These foods require the lowest effort. Nuts, grains, seeds, and insects are next on the pyramid and can offer slightly more calories but also take more effort to collect. Fish, mollusks, crustaceans, and bird eggs are a good trade-off between the calories you burn while collecting them and the calories they return when eaten. Mushrooms, reptiles, and amphibians will take more time, consideration, and effort to collect, catch, and process; however, they can be a filling and satiating meal. At the top of the food pyramid are small game, birds, and large game—which will require some ingenuity, patience, and effort on your part but can help sustain you for a long time if you are successful. The base of the pyramid should be your priority. Only consider the successive layers if you have built up a strong foundation as a fallback. This means having stores of food that you can rely on if your hunts are not successful.

INDEX

Berries

Blackberries: aggregates of small black berries that grow on prickly brambles; very sweet, juicy, and safe to eat straight from the plant

Blueberries: waxy blue with a five-pointed crow that grows on woody shrubs in colder and temperate regions

Bunchberry: bright red berries with one or two large seeds growing close to the ground in shady forests

Cloudberry: tightly-packed clumps of small orange-amber berries growing on creeping rhizomes in cooler regions

Cranberries: red, oblong-shaped berries growing on low-lying, creeping shrubs in acidic soils near bogs and marshes

Gooseberries: orange berries each enclosed in a protective sheath of thin leaves, growing on small, spiny bushes; can tolerate very cold climates

Elderberries: small, black berries growing in red stems in large groups on small shrubs or trees (The ripe berries are only edible once cooked.)

Mulberries: oblong aggregates of very tiny black berries filled with dark juice growing on small- or medium-sized shrubs

Raspberries: hollow aggregates of small, red berries growing on prickle-covered shrubs

Salmon Berries: aggregates of small red-orange berries with several soft spines and a spinous crown on the fruit, growing on shrubs with sparse spines

Wild Strawberries: red berries similar to commercial strawberries but smaller and rounder, with more prominent seeds, growing on low-growing, creeping runners

Fruit

Hawthorn Apples: red and apple-like fruits but usually as small as berries growing on trees and woody shrubs with thorny branches; found in northern, temperate regions

Mayapple Fruits: medium-sized, oblong, green-yellow fleshy fruits resembling limes; grows close to the ground underneath two leaves

Persimmon: medium yellow to orange fruits with large brown seeds growing on trees in northern, temperate regions

Prickly Pear Cactus: pear-sized fruits; green and turn red when ripe, growing on spine-covered cactus plants in arid and semi-arid regions

Wild Apple: medium-sized, apple-like fruits domesticated to produce commercial apples (They are quite similar to each other.); red to yellow skins and fleshy insides growing on trees.

Wild Black Cherry: medium-sized, shiny black fruits with stone seeds and long stems growing on trees

Wild Grape: similar to commercial grapes with round, black fruits, and waxy skins growing on vines in large groups

Wild Greens, Shoots, and Flowers

Amaranth: low-growing, broad-leaf plants with bright, red-pink flowers growing in clusters of spikes

Asparagus: resembling commercial asparagus with short, tough stems and modified, flowering tips that can grow in several types of habitats

Bamboo: evergreen grass; grows thick, woody, and hollow stems with distinct nodes along the length

Bull Kelp: Pacific coast seaweed with a long stalk, bulbous float and several flowing leaves

Burdock: low-growing plant with a rosette of very large leaves and thistle-like flowers (The leaves are hairy and have undulating margins.)

Catnip: shrubby plant with small, heart-shaped leaves covered in fine hair and releases distinctive aroma when crushed

Cattails: grassy plant with long, sword-like leaves and flowering stems with sausage shape near the tip; grows near waters of wetlands, rivers, lakes, and streams

Chickweed: very small, leafy, and stringy plant growing close to the ground; leaves are opposite with small flowers made up of five pairs of white petals

Chicory: rosette of long, toothy, and hairy leaves with thick midribs and blue-purple flowers with distinct toothy-tipped petals

Clovers: very small herbaceous plant with leaves divided into three leaflets, usually round or heart-shaped; small flowers with tubular petals either red, pink, or white

Coltsfoot: low-growing with medium, shallowly lobed and toothed leaves with white hairs on the underside and bright yellow flowers with thin petals

Coneflower: short stems with sparsely-toothed sword-shaped leaves (The flowers have a central spiny cone structure surrounded by pink petals.)

Curly Dock: low rosette of long, narrow, and hairless leaves with wavy edges and stalks of tiny red-crimson flowers growing in clumps

Dandelions: a ubiquitous weed with low-growing rosette of long, toothy, and lobed leaves with thick midribs. (The flowers are yellow and develop a white puffball.)

Dulse: small, flat, red seaweed that grows with irregularly branching lobes

Fiddlehead Ferns: young ferns that grow on smooth green stalks that end in a spiraled "fiddlehead," usually covered in very fine hairs

Fireweed: a tall, herbaceous plant growing as erect stems with smooth, lance-shaped, alternating leaves; stems are tipped with bright pink flowers

Garlic Mustard: a low-lying, erect plant with broad kidney- or heart-shaped leaves that have scalloped edges and small flowers with four white petals

Greenbrier: a woody vine, sometimes shrub, covered in spines and tendrils, with smooth and shiny heart-shaped leaves that grows in thickets and woods

Green Seaweed: includes many different kinds of green seaweed and algal growths found in marine environments (All are safe for eating.)

Henbit: a small, weedy plant with rosettes of leaves at each node of the short stem. Leaves are scalloped, heart-shaped, and aromatic (Small pink, tubular flowers grow at the top of the stem.)

Kelp: includes many kinds of marine plants that grow on long stalks with either green or reddish-brown leaves and bulbous floats

Lamb's Quarters: small stems with pale green, triangular leaves with scalloped margins and small, bulbous, pale-yellow flowers at the top

Milkweed: medium-sized plants with erect stems and long, sword-shaped leaves with smooth margins.

Produce distinctive white sap and have spherical globes of several pinkish flowers; must be cooked

Miner's Lettuce: a low-growing, slightly succulent, plant with medium-sized, round, and disk-like leaves—each growing from a basal stem; distinct as the stem passes directly through the leaf; flowers also grow in the center of the leaf.

Mullein: a medium plant with single, unbranching stem with a thick rosette of basal leaves that become smaller upward on the stem. The leaves are oval and covered in very fine, gray hairs with yellow flowers growing near the top.

Pickleweed: small, succulent plant that grows near salty marshes, estuaries, and mangroves (The jointed stems are covered in scale-like leaves and reddish, jointed flower-structures grow at the tips.)

Plantain: medium to large; broadly oval leaves grow on the ground in a rosette with small flower spikes growing from the center.

Purslane: small plant with succulent leaves and stems that forms spreading mats. (The leaves are paddle-shaped and stems sometimes have a reddish color.)

Queen Anne's Lace (Wild Carrot): a medium plant with tall, thin stems and lacy, fern-like leaves (Several tiny white flowers form a flat-topped, umbrella-shaped cluster.) Be careful not to confuse it with poison hemlock, which is nearly identical, but instead of one neatly packed cluster of flowers, it has several smaller clusters that are more spread out. Roots can also be eaten.

Sea Lettuce: type of green algae that forms lobed, leafy structures that grow on rocks in marine environments. They are transparent, delicate, and slimy.

Sheep Sorrel: a medium plant with basal leaves and erect stems that branch slightly at the top. The leaves are smooth and oblong but with two small lobes at the base which form an arrow-like shape. Tiny red flowers grow on the tips of spikes.

Stinging Nettle: herbaceous plant with erect stems and leaves that grow alternately up the stem, becoming smaller near the top. The leaves are triangular and serrated, and small flower spikes grow from the nodes. The stems and leaves are covered in fine, stinging hairs.

Sumac: a small tree or shrub with small, pinnate leaves and sword-shaped leaflets. Leaves are arranged spirally around the branches and bright red flowers grow in thick, spike-like clusters.

Sweet Gale: a shrub with long, oblong leaves that have toothed tips but mostly smooth side margins and a sweet aroma. The leaves are quite resinous, and the plant grows in boggy, acidic areas.

Violets: small plant with basal rosette of leaves that each have long stalks. Leaves are heart- or oval-shaped with scalloped edges. Flowers are vibrant violet in color with five petals.

Watercress: a small and aquatic plant with many round leaflets growing from short, juicy stems, often forming mats. The leaves have a fresh, peppery taste.

Water Lily: aquatic plants with characteristic circular leaves that float on the surface of water bodies. Flowers have several pointed petals. (Only the yellow and fragrant (white) water lilies are edible, being identified by their flower color.)

Wild Leek: an early spring plant growing low to the ground with a few long, smooth leaves, reddish stems and a white bulb covered in short white hair-like roots (The leaves and bulb have a strong, onion-like smell.)

Wood Lily: medium-sized plant with a single erect stem with whorls of long, slender leaves along the nodes; red flower with six pointed petals at the top of the stem

Wood Sorrel: small weedy plant very similar to clovers except that each of the three heart-shaped leaflets has a fold down the center; flowers are usually yellow with five petals.

Yarrow: medium-sized plant with erect stems and sparse leaves. Leaves are pinnate with several, very fine leaflets on either side of the prominent midrib, each being further divided and deeply lobed. Small flowers grow in flat-topped or dome-shaped clusters at the top of the stem. It can be confused with poison hemlock, but the leaves are much smaller and very delicate in comparison.

Tubers and Roots

Cattail Root: thick horizontal rhizomes of the cattail plant identified by its long reed-like grasses and sausage-like flower structure

Daylily Root: several, basal, long, smooth, and slender leaves with reddish-orange, bell-shaped flowers each with five petals (The thick, fleshy roots can be harvested for eating.)

Jerusalem Artichoke: a tall plant with erect stems; elongated, triangular leaves; and yellow flowers; thick and tuberous roots, almost like ginger

Wild Garlic: a small plant with long, smooth basal leaves that droop and small stalks with white flowers (The roots form small, elongated bulbs that can be eaten.)

Wild Ginger: a low-growing plant with heart-shaped leaves found on forest floors; forms long, fibrous roots that can be eaten

Wild Onions: grows from a thick underground bulb, forming long blade-like basal leaves and spherical clusters of purple or white flowers

Nuts

Acorns: nuts of oak trees; tough, fibrous covering and a woody cup, enclosing the fleshy meat; must be cooked

Beech Nuts: nuts of beech trees; grow in spinous capsules that split open into four to reveal four oblong, pointed meaty nuts

Chestnut: nuts of the chestnut tree; covered in a protective coating with hairy burs, with three to four dark brown, round nuts inside.

Chinquapin: the nut from a type of chestnut tree (The coating is covered in burs, usually light green in color, with a single dark brown nut inside.)

Hazelnut: from the hazel tree; grow in a hard, woody husk with a pale white cap and a fleshy nut inside

Hickory: from the hickory tree; grow inside hard, woody husks which split open into four parts to reveal an undulated nut inside

Macadamia: from the macadamia tree and more common in tropical areas; have a spherical husk revealing a pale and round nut inside

Pecan: from the pecan tree; have a relatively thin but woody husk and break open to reveal two undulated, brain-like nuts which are quite soft

Pine Nuts: found in the scales of pine cones from many kinds of pine trees (They are small and pointed.)

Walnut: from walnut trees; very tough and protected by a thick, woody husk which can be cracked open to reveal the brain-like nuts and soft nuts inside

Seeds and Grains

Chia Seeds: grow from a small, herby plant with erect stems, heart-shaped serrated leaves, and small, tubular purple flowers (The seeds are very small and black.)

Dock Seeds: from the curly dock plant; seeds are reddish brown, covered in papery wings, and have pointed tips

Gama Grass: This is a common grass with long, spear-shaped leaves with parallel veins growing from the base. The seeds are sheathed in segments at the top of the flowering stalk.

Indian Rice Grass: grows as long, round stalks with delicate, slightly branching, flower heads at the top and produces a few small, elongated brown seeds with pointed tips

Mesquite Pods: seed pods from the mesquite tree with delicate, fern-like bipinnate leaves divided into about 40 narrow leaflets. Seed pods contain a single row of 20 to 30 seeds.

Milkweed Pods: For these pods, several dozen seeds grow on a spiny, pointed capsule, and each seed is covered in a feathery pappus.

Sunflower Seeds: Growing in the central disk of sunflowers in large numbers, the pointed seeds are contained in husks which can be cracked open.

Wild Barnyard Grass: Also known as wild millet, the grass grows with long round stalks and a few blade-like leaves. The seeds grow in stocky clusters at the top of the stalks.

Wild Rice: grows in moist areas with long blades and round stalks; the seeds are rice grains, growing at the top of the stalks. (They droop under the weight.)

Wild Rye: very similar to wheat with long cylindrical stalks and a few blade-like leaves (The seeds grow on the top of the stalks which have long, thin filaments.)

Insects

Ant Larvae: They can be found wherever ants are found. They are small, white, and grub-like and only inside the ant nests.

Ants: These are ubiquitous in almost every environment and found in abundance within their nests. Some ants dig burrows, others build hills or mounds, and some ants live in thorny trees.

Aphids: Aphids can be found on vegetation where they drink sap. Look for them on the softer parts of different plants—especially near the nodes, stems, and flowers.

Beetle Larvae: Large, whitish, and worm-like, beetle larvae often have small dark heads and sometimes with legs. They are soft and fleshy and can be found in moist soils, under leaf litter, or in rotting wood.

Beetles: Coming in a massive variety of sizes, shapes and colors, beetles all have hard exoskeletons which protect their wings and bodies. They can be found in many kinds of habitats.

Crickets: have two pairs of wings; thin, tapering bodies; and large hind legs for jumping (Crickets live in moist, warm environments like under leaf debris.)

Earwigs: large and elongated insects with distinctive forceps and pincer structures on their behinds (They can be found in dark, moist places with lots of water.)

Grasshoppers: similar to crickets but often much larger and more commonly found in drier and grassy habitats

Maggots: the larvae of flies which are laid as eggs in rotting organic matter, hatching and developing into maggots; can grow quite large

Termites: These are similar in appearance to ants but often lighter in color with larger heads. They feed on wood and are found in habitats with lots of woody material, often building their nest inside trees or constructing large and tall termite mounds.

Woodlice: This is a type of crustacean found on land, also known as rolly polly bug, pill bugs, or sow bugs.

They have many armored segments which can be used to roll up into a tight ball. They live in moist soils, under rotting wood, and leaf litter.

Fish, Mollusks, and Crustaceans

Clams: These are bivalves with two equally-sized shells that close on one side using a strong muscle. They are found in many marine environments but especially tidal zones.

Crabs: Crabs are crustaceans with one main body unit and five pairs of limbs all protected by a hard exoskeleton. One pair of front limbs is a strong set of claws. Crabs live in freshwater and marine environments and can be found running along sandy banks and beaches.

Fish: There are thousands of different fish species in freshwater, marine, and brackish environments. They have scaled skin and streamlined bodies with various sets of fins.

Limpets: Limpets are a kind of mollusk with a single, flattened, conical shell that attaches to rocks in marine and tidal environments. They are usually quite small, but some can grow much larger. They are very strong and can be tricky to remove from rocks.

Lobster: This is a type of crustacean with a long, muscular tail; large front claws; and long antennae.

Lobsters and crayfish are very similar, but they live in different environments—lobsters are marine while crayfish live in freshwater. They can usually be found in rocky, aquatic habitats.

Mussels: These are bivalves with two black, tear-drop-shaped shells that are held tightly together by a strong muscle. They live in freshwater and marine environments, usually attached to rocks where water flows most of the time. They do not do well when exposed to air.

Octopus: These cephalopods ("head foot") have eight tentacles and a large central head, existing only in marine environments. They are most commonly observed in tidal and rocky pools but also exist in open waters. They have sharp, biting beaks on their underside.

Oysters: These are bivalves similar to mussels with a teardrop shape, though some are more rounded; however, they have quite a rough and pearly texture. They are most common in brackish waters where freshwater meets marine water like estuaries—where they attach to rocks, piers and other stationary objects.

Periwinkles: small to medium marine snails that can be found attached to rocks

Shrimp: occurring in freshwater and marine environments and similar to lobsters but much smaller and without strong claws (They have softer exoskeletons and are usually found in large groups.)

Squid: This is a type of cephalopod with an elongated head, eight arms, and two tentacles. They have very soft bodies with a single internal shell that supports their organs—most commonly found in open oceans and deep seas.

Urchin: This is a member of the starfish family that has a hard, round, near spherical shell through which several spines poke through. The underside has a mouth in the center. They most often appear as a ball of spikes and are found in coral reefs, tidal pools, and rocky marine environments.

Mushrooms

Boletes: similar shape to typical button mushrooms but slightly larger, with pale pores and a spongy appearance on the underside of the cap—not gills; typically pale brown, whitish, or yellowish—not blue; found growing near the roots of large trees like oaks

Chanterelles: yellowish and trumpet shaped with false gills on the underside of the cap that are more like forked wrinkles that run partially down the stem; solid and pale white inside of the stem; often found in conifer forests

Chicken of the Woods: soft, spongy, and yellowish-orange brackets that grow horizontally in clusters on the sides of trees (The edges are pale yellow while the inner part is orange.)

Corn Smut: a fungus that infects the individual kernels of a corn cob, developing enlarged, gray galls which are edible

Hen of the Woods: This is a slightly firm mushroom made up of a cluster of several leafy fronds, like the ruffles of a sitting hen. They are usually dark brown, sometimes pale brown, or orange and grow near the bases of oak trees.

Honey Mushroom: small to medium-sized clusters of flat-capped mushrooms with a honey-orange color (though often brown as well)—the top of the cap is covered in a fine fuzz, and the underside is covered in gills that run partially down the stem until it reaches the "ring" which is like a skirt.

Lion's Mane: This is a pale white mushroom that grows long, cascading "teeth" that look like the shaggy mane of a lion. They are also described as looking like icicles hanging from the central stalk. They are quite distinctive and typically grow on dead or rotting logs.

Lobster Mushroom: These are very similar to chanterelles but more prized. They have a much brighter red color like a lobster but with a trumpet-shaped cap. The underside has false gills, and the inside of the stalk is a pale white color; they're found near the base of trees, especially hemlocks.

Milk Caps: a large, pale to reddish brown mushroom with a convex-shaped cap; underside has true gills which release a milky white sap when cut or broken

Morel Mushrooms: distinctive mushroom with a slightly conical-shaped cap covered in wrinkles and pits; can be dark to pale brown; cap and the stalk must be hollow (False morels are similarly poisonous but distinguished by being solid inside.) They grow on the ground near large trees.

Oyster Mushroom: white oyster- or fan-shaped caps that grow on the side of hardwood trees in a shelf-like fashion; underside of the cap is covered in gills that run down the stem

Puffball: These are small to large mushrooms that can be identified easily because they have no gills and are bright white inside. Their caps attach smoothly to the stalks with no clear separation. The top of the cap may be smooth, slightly cracked, or covered in fine, hair-like structures.

Reptiles and Amphibians

Turtles: turtles live in aquatic environments, having a large, thick shell and four flippers. Some species can retract into their shells while most larger species cannot.

Snakes: snakes are long, slithering reptiles with no legs. Most snakes are dangerous, either being able to bite, constrict or inject venom. They are very muscular and must be treated with care. Similar animals include legless skinks which, in terms of eating, can be treated in the same way.

Frogs and toads: amphibians found in many types of habitats with long muscular legs for jumping (Frogs are usually found in moist or aquatic environments while toads can survive in drier environments.)

Salamanders: This is a lizard-like amphibian with porous skin that can be found in aquatic freshwater environments.

Birds and Small Game

Chipmunk: This is a type of squirrel native to North America identified by the stripes down their backs. They live in many habitats including woodlands, forests, and plains; They are also quite solitary.

Cranes: medium to large flying birds that spend most of their time near aquatic habitats hunting fish (They have long legs but short necks and lack webbing on their toes.)

Ducks: small aquatic birds with webbed feet, short legs, and short necks; will always be found near water and feed on fish, as well as seeds, algae, and other floating debris; generally social and live in groups

Geese: Geese are similar to ducks but larger with longer legs and necks. They are also social and live in large groups.

Grouse and Ptarmigan: These are small, chicken-like birds with brown, often spotty feathers. Ptarmigans turn pure white during winter where they live in snowy habitats. They are generally solitary birds.

Hares and Rabbits: These are medium-sized rodents with characteristic long, pointed ears and jumping locomotion. Hares are typically larger and can be found in drier habitats while rabbits are small and live in forests and woodlands. Rabbits typically dig burrows where they live in groups, while hares dig small depressions in long, grassy areas and are solitary.

Herons: similar to a crane except with long necks

Mice: small to tiny rodents with pointed, whiskered snouts; round ears; and a long, scaly tail; typically found in grassy habitats where they feed on seeds; most often found alone but live in breeding groups

Pigeons: These are small, plump birds with small bills common in cities but also in various wild habitats. Their heads bob back and forth as they walk, and they are good fliers. Their feathers sometimes shimmer around their necks, and they have stripes on their wings.

Quail: small, chicken-like birds with plump bodies, striped feathers, and often sporting decoration on their heads; prized for their meat and eggs; live on the ground in grasslands, woodlands, and arid savannas (They are also solitary or live in pairs.)

Squirrel: These are medium-sized rodents with long, bushy tails that live in trees. They create caches of nuts and seeds to last them over winters which can be exploited. Several species exist, but the red and gray squirrels are most common. Gray squirrels are much larger and more aggressive.

Swans: Swans are large water birds with long, graceful necks, long legs, and webbed feet. They are typically white with a black ridge across their brows and bright orange bills. They are most commonly found in pairs and can be very aggressive—using the sharp spurs on their legs to defend themselves.

Wild turkey: These are large, chicken-like birds that live in North America. They live on the ground and are able to fly but rarely do. They are usually dark or black in color—sporting fleshy red wattles and blue faces. Males often display their back feathers in a large, attractive fan, and they have a distinctive "gobble" call.

Large Game

Caribou and Reindeer: large and stocky deer with large, branching antlers (The antlers are found on males and females.) Their noses are protected by white hairs, and they do not migrate. Caribou and reindeer are the same species but are found in different places. Caribou live in North America, whereas reindeer live in Europe and Asia.

Elk: a very large deer with antlers smaller than caribou and only occurring on males (They have naked noses and migrate over large distances each season.)

Moose: the largest deer in the world with thick, rounded snouts and beards—their antlers are very large and branching, but unlike elk or caribou, they are more shovel-like with flat pieces. Females do not grow antlers. Moose do not migrate very large distances, though they do move between nearby areas.

White-tailed deer: a medium-sized deer with branching antlers and their tails are distinctively white tails on the underside. (They have black noses and white bellies.)

Wild boar: resembling domestic pigs except with long brown fur, sharp tusk-like teeth, and a more hunched posture; sometimes have a black mane along their necks and spines. (Baby boars have a striped pattern on their fur.)

CONCLUSION

"Only those who will risk going too far can possibly find out how far one can go"

— T.S. ELIOT

All that nature has to offer is right at your fingertips, and with the knowledge and skills you have learned, you will be able to tackle any challenge that comes your way. Nature provides everything you could possibly need—not only to survive but to thrive and to reach your true potential.

This book has looked at some practical foraging survival skills that can help you overcome an unexpected event in the wilderness. You should know, understand, and appreciate some of the most essential rules of a forager:

1. Be aware of your surroundings.
2. Never go alone.
3. Protect yourself.
4. Try to avoid uncertainty by being prepared.
5. Do not take unnecessary risks.
6. Create a mental list of the local edible foods in your region.
7. Do your research and consult guidebooks.
8. Always wash your food.
9. Always cook your food.
10. Always carry out a universal edibility test if you are in doubt.
11. Be a sustainable forager that cares about endangered and threatened species.
12. Know which parts of a plant are safe to eat.
13. Exploit the seasons by harvesting the best edibles at different times of year.
14. Respect the dangers of plant poisons.
15. Do not be afraid to eat insects.
16. Avoid bright colors.
17. Do not be afraid to eat slimy creatures.
18. Opt for small game over large game.
19. Avoid diseased and sick edibles.

20. Avoid areas contaminated by human activity.
21. Exploit the vast plethora of resources provided by the ocean.
22. Do not forget to get enough vitamins and minerals.
23. Do not trespass.
24. Share what you have learned.

Chapter 1 provided a comprehensive guide into some of the best types of edibles to look out for, namely the tree nuts, seeds, roots, tubers, berries, and fruit which are all provided by plants. They require very little effort to collect and give you the essential nutrients you need to stay alert, healthy, and alive.

Some of the most common edible plants you may come across—not only in the wilderness but also in urban areas—include prickly pears, morel mushrooms, chickweed, dandelions, raspberries, blackberries, and blueberries, chicken of the woods mushrooms, amaranth, cattails, and chanterelle mushrooms. These foods often grow in great abundance; they are hardy and tough, thriving in several different kinds of environments across the Northern Hemisphere. However, don't forget the important tips to remember when you struggle to find edible plants. Plants will always need water to survive, and they have many ingenious ways to find it. Look to rocky outcrops and valleys and near the edges of forests where plants are protected.

In Chapter 2, we looked into how to go about identifying plants. Knowing some basic tips and tricks can help save a lot of time and energy. Try to keep reading up on botanical terminologies such as the shape of leaves, the type of veins, and the shape of their margins. Keep in mind the most common plant families:

- The conifer trees have thick, woody trunks and needle or scale-like leaves that grow in colder climates across the world. They reproduce using cones that have edible nuts inside. Conifers can also be used for their several medicinal properties.
- The daisy family is made up of some of the most prominent flowers in the world, including daisies and sunflowers. They are always easily recognizable by their flowers which have a central disk surrounded by petals.
- The grass family comprises several thousand species, making up one of the world's most important sources of food. All grains come from the tiny flowers sitting on top of the grass stalks. Grasses most commonly grow in drier habitats.
- Ferns and their relatives are an ancient type of

plant that does not produce flowers, instead relying on spores for reproduction. Their young fiddleheads can provide a valuable source of nourishment when you find yourself in a woodland or forest without food.

- The mint family encompasses several small flowering plants. They all have highly aromatic leaves, are almost always triangular, and have serrated edges.

- The mustard family contains quite a few edible plants and can easily be identified by their X- or H-shaped flowers.

- The parsley family is a tricky group containing several poisonous species that closely resemble edible species. They have lacy leaves and flowers growing in umbrella-like clusters.

- The pea family, similar to parsley, contains several edible plants as well as toxic varieties. They are also easy to identify, having distinct flowers and producing seeds in pods.

Even with all of these identification tips, there are also more rules to keep in mind. As previously mentioned, you should try to avoid eating plants from urban or industrial areas where they may have been exposed to chemical pollutants. Avoid plants that smell strongly of almond, as this indicates the presence of cyanide; also, avoid bitter-tasting or soapy plants. Avoid most plants with milky or discolored sap and try to stay away from unidentified legumes, beans, or seed pods which are often toxic. Most plants in the parsley family are quite dangerous as well. Avoid plants that have physical defenses like spurs, spines, or thorns. Also, only eat mushrooms if you absolutely have to and if you are completely certain that they are a safe variety.

The universal edibility test is a useful but long and drawn-out process. You should always opt for plants that you can identify with certainty, but when no other options are available, this is a reliable method for ensuring you do not consume poisonous plants. The main steps of the edibility test include locating plants that are actually abundant and could nourish you, separating them into their different parts, and working with only one part at a time. Then, testing the plant by consuming small quantities and applying it to the skin to detect any amount of irritation will also help. If the plants are able to pass these tests, you can safely rely on them when out in the wilderness, but be sure you note their definition characteristics including habitat, size, appearance, smell, and taste.

It is critical to remember some of the most common look-alikes you may come across in the wilderness. Always refer back to the table provided in Chapter 2 in case of doubt to avoid confusing moonseeds with wild grapes or true morels with false morels.

Chapter 3 began to delve into one of the most life-saving skills someone in the wilderness can have—how to build a fire. This skill involves the ability to identify and collect suitable materials for starting and maintaining a fire, as well as important aspects of fire safety. Fires require tinder, kindling, and firewood in order to burn successfully in a survival situation without access to paraffin or other flammable chemicals. We also covered several fire designs, such as the teepee, the log cabin, and the star design—which all have different advantages and disadvantages depending on your needs. Some types of fires are better suited to cooking and providing high heat, whereas others are better at surviving for longer periods of time.

Knowing how to start a fire without access to a lighter or matches is critical. You can collect all the firewood in the world, and it will be useless without a spark to ignite it. There are several tried-and-tested methods used by humans all over the world for tens of thousands of years, like the hand drill or fire plow. However, we should always try to be adaptable as possible and know how to use and implement many other methods including the bow drill; flint and steel; using lenses and sunlight; and mirrors or electricity so that you can always start a fire no matter what environment or condition you may find yourself in.

We also discussed some of the plants that absolutely must be cooked before eating. As a general rule, you should try to cook all the wild edibles you find in nature for safety reasons. Clovers, stinging nettles, acorns, cattail roots, whole violets, plantain leaves, kelp, and bamboo should all be thoroughly boiled or cooked over a fire. All animal foods must also be cooked to rid them of parasites.

Chapter 4 looked into some of the ways that you can produce all the amenities you need from nature, including tools, utensils, water containers, cooking containers, cooking apparatus, and weapons. Rocks serve as a valuable raw material for constructing sharp blades if you have the patience to work them, and knowing how to turn plant fibers into strong ropes can help you escape tricky situations. Weapons not only serve as a defense against predators and territorial animals but can be used to hunt, skin, and prepare prey. Utensils, though not completely necessary, help people in a survival situation by lifting their morale and dignity, and eating out of a bowl or a plate is also much more hygienic than eating from the floor.

Transporting water is a major challenge in the wild, but there are several options available to you including wooden implements, bamboo, gourds, seed pods and leaves, and also various animal parts like intestines or bladders. This chapter also discussed some of the ways you can cook your food using a fire, stove, grill, or oven. Solar cooking is a great way to cook not only in a survival situation, but is also something you should try at home. It requires no electricity and can produce some delectable dishes.

Chapter 4 also discussed water; the importance of safe, clean, drinking water; how to find it; and how to purify it. You can find water in almost any habitat, including forests, deserts, grasslands, savannas, mountains, and even coastal habitats—you just need to know where to look. Water stills are one of the easiest and most effective ways to extract water from the environment when you cannot find any on the surface, and they also serve as a way to purify your water of toxins, chemicals, and parasites. Water filtration is another important aspect to consider, and you can easily make highly effective filters using nothing but raw, natural materials.

Preparedness and safety was the final highlight of this chapter, emphasizing the need to take care when working with fire and hot objects, as you will not have access to medical care. It is also important to remember that you are not alone when out in wild environments, and there are many dangerous animals who may try to steal your hard-earned foods or defend their territories against you. Be wary, secure your food, and use weapons and fire as a defense.

In Chapter 5, we delved into some unconventional edibles, namely insects. Insects are abundant in most habitats, and many various groups are completely safe to eat. Grasshoppers, crickets, ants, termites, grubs, beetles, and many other types of bugs are an excellent choice if you can overcome the crunchy texture. Though many of us would prefer a juicy rabbit or piece of deer meat, insects can provide just as much fat and protein with half the effort. Of course, there are some types of creepy crawlies that are best avoided, including spiders and scorpions. However, with some care and skill, these too can make a great meal in the wilderness. As always, try to avoid those with bright coloration, as they are often poisonous.

Moving on from the smaller critters, Chapter 6 provided an introduction to hunting larger animals. One of the main takeaways from this section should be that catching prey animals is difficult; it takes a lot of time and energy; and there is never any guarantee of success. You must always try to balance out your efforts with the potential rewards and the consequences of failure. However, there are many skills that can improve your chances, such as tracking animals by their footprints, identifying signs of activity, and setting up traps in opportune areas. Traps are a great, low-energy alternative to having to chase down an animal with a spear or net. There are many inventive designs suited to different kinds of prey that can significantly reduce the amount of energy you need to spend in catching a decent dinner. You should try to construct your own traps at home to see if they are effective!

Finally, Chapter 7 summarized some of the most important wild edibles you are likely to come across. Use this index whenever you are uncertain about a wild edible. It is critical to keep in mind the survival food pyramid, and you need to always ensure that you focus on foraging for foods that are abundant and easy to collect. Time and energy are your most valuable resources, and you cannot afford to waste them in a survival situation where your life is on the line. You can safely rely on the wide range of plants and insects before attempting to catch small animals. Reptiles, amphibians, and eggs from birds are generally much easier to capture compared to birds or small mammals, and large game should be saved for those times when you have already built up a good stock of not only alternative foods but other resources like firewood and water.

I hope this book will serve you well in your adventures. With the tools, tips, and tricks you've learned throughout this book, it is my hope that you can begin harnessing your foraging knowledge and skills—not only out in the wilderness but also in your local regions and backyards. See if you can identify the plants you come across in your travels; maybe keep a journal or log of the type of plants you find. Don't turn down the chance to eat insects: You never know just how tasty they might be! Lastly, practice your fire-starting abilities with the tips left for you.

Please be sure to leave a review if you enjoyed this book!

Practical Survival Skills Shows You How To Make Fire Without Matches

- Learn a skill as old as mankind & gain confidence in your survival chances.
- Be the one to help yourself & others with these skills in a fraught situation.
- Learn how mother nature always provides a way & is abundant in provisions.
- Improve your knowledge with this free fire making guide.

As a thank you for choosing this book. Have a free download on J.P. Logan. Grab my Fire Making Guide: Just visit jploganbooks.com to download your FREE copy now!

REFERENCES

Ahmad, R. S., Imran, A., & Hussain, M. B. (2018). Nutritional composition of meat. In *www.intechopen.com*. IntechOpen. https://www.intechopen.com/chapters/61245

All images are courtesy of Pixabay and Unsplash.

Anderberg, J. (2016, April 20). *How to find water in the wild*. The Art of Manliness. https://www.artofmanliness.com/skills/outdoor-survival/how-to-find-water-in-the-wild/

Angier, B. (2016). *How to eat in the woods: A complete guide to foraging, trapping, fishing, and finding sustenance in the wild*. Black Dog & Leventhal.

Backcountry Chronicles. (n.d.). *Wilderness survival rules of 3 - air, shelter, water & food.* www.backcountrychronicles.com. https://www.backcountrychronicles.com/wilderness-survival-rules-of-3/

Bennett, J. (2016, December 8). *Everything you need to know about foraging for food in the wild.* Popular Mechanics. https://www.popularmechanics.com/adventure/outdoors/tips/a24203/eat-forage-food-wild-alone-history-channel/

Brindle, D. (2020, August 15). *7 DIY survival traps to know.* ReThinkSurvival.com. https://rethinksurvival.com/7-diy-survival-traps-to-know/

Brown, T., & Morgan, B. (n.d.). *How to track animals in the wilderness.* Mother Earth News. Retrieved October 11, 2021, from https://www.motherearthnews.com/nature-and-environment/how-to-track-animals-in-the-wilderness-zmaz82sozgoe

Bryant, C. W. (2008, April 21). *What is the universal edibility test?* HowStuffWorks. https://adventure.howstuffworks.com/universal-edibility-test.htm

Burns, J. (2016, May 16). *8 edible plants with potentially deadly doppelgängers.* Mentalfloss. https://www.mentalfloss.com/article/69254/8-edible-plants-potentially-deadly-doppelgangers

Canterbury, D. (2016). *The bushcraft field guide to trapping, gathering, & cooking in the wild.* Adams Media.

Cipriani, P. (2020, March 25). *Survival hunting tips.* Wilderness Awareness School. https://www. wildernessawareness.org/articles/survival-hunting-tips/

Coelho, S. (2019, February 22). *50 edible wild plants you can forage for a free meal.* MorningChores. https:// morningchores.com/edible-wild-plants/

Cowan, D. (2020, March 25). *How to make a survival water filter.* Wilderness Awareness School. https:// www.wildernessawareness.org/articles/how-to-make-a-survival-water-filter/

Cozzens, B. (2018). *Bodies of water in the grasslands.* Sciencing. https://sciencing.com/bodies-water-grasslands-7464691.html

DNews. (2011, August 5). *How to find clean water in the jungle.* Seeker. https://www.seeker.com/how-to-find-clean-water-in-the-jungle-1765355301.html

Dodrill, T. (2020, March 16). *Foraging for survival: The ultimate guide.* Survival Sullivan. https://www. survivalsullivan.com/survival-foraging/

Dotson, R. (2018, August 17). *Identifying wild edibles.* Survival Dispatch. https://survivaldispatch.com/how-to-increase-your-food-supply-with-wild-edibles/

Dr. Seuss Quotes. (n.d.). BrainyQuote.com. Retrieved October 19, 2021, from BrainyQuote.com Web site: https://www.brainyquote.com/quotes/dr_seuss_597901

Emergency Essentials. (2017, March). *Survival 101: Foraging for edible plants.* Be Prepared. https://beprepared.com/blogs/articles/survival-101-foraging-for-edible-plants

Fair, J. (2020, January 14). *Apex predators in the wild: which mammals are the most dangerous?* Discover Wildlife. https://www.discoverwildlife.com/animal-facts/mammals/hunting-success-rates-how-predators-compare/

Finding Food in the Wilderness. (n.d.). Crisistimes.com. http://crisistimes.com/survival_food.php

Frank Lloyd Wright Quotes. (n.d.). BrainyQuote.com. Retrieved October 19, 2021, from BrainyQuote.com Web site: https://www.brainyquote.com/quotes/frank_lloyd_wright_127707

Guest Authors. (2017, November). *Foraging for beginners: Tips for safely gathering wild, edible foods.* Gore-Tex.

https://www.gore-tex.com/blog/foraging-food-wild-plants

Hawke, D. (2019). *Foraging for survival: edible wild plants of North America*. Skyhorse.

Hill, D. (2018, April 25). *How to identify edible plants - an introduction*. Gone Feral. https://www.goneferal.org/identify-edible-plants-introduction/

Hodgkins, K., & Cage, C. (2017). *16 best edible insects*. Greenbelly Meals. https://www.greenbelly.co/pages/edible-insects

Hunter, J. (2016, August 26). *5 ridiculously simple animal traps and snares for outdoor survival*. Primal Survivor. https://www.primalsurvivor.net/simple-animal-traps-snares/

John Muir Quotes. (n.d.). BrainyQuote.com. https://www.brainyquote.com/quotes/john_muir_108391

Josh Gale. (2011, April 18). *Survival skill #1 – Make fire*. Wilderness Magazine. https://wildernessmag.co.nz/survival-skill-1-make-fire/

Knight, J. (n.d.). *Building a fire pit*. Alderleaf Wilderness College. https://www.wildernesscollege.com/building-a-fire-pit.html

Laylin, T. (2016, March 28). *Edible insects: The alternative protein people are buzzing about.* PartSelect.com. https://www.fix.com/blog/edible-insects/

Louv, M. (2018, June 27). *12 edible bugs that could help you survive.* Backpacker. https://www.backpacker.com/survival/12-edible-bugs-that-could-help-you-survive/

Macwelch, T. (2014, July 1). *Survival skills: build a cage fish trap.* Outdoor Life. https://www.outdoorlife.com/blogs/survivalist/2014/06/survival-skills-build-cage-fish-trap/

Macwelch, T. (2019a, January 23). *Survival skills: 3 ways to make a wooden bowl in the wild Tim Macwelch.* Outdoor Life. https://www.outdoorlife.com/blogs/survivalist/survival-skills-3-ways-make-wooden-bowl-wild/

Macwelch, T. (2019b, January 23). *Survival skills: Animal tracking 101.* Outdoor Life. https://www.outdoorlife.com/blogs/survivalist/2012/03/survival-skills-animal-tracking-101/

MacWelch, T. (2019, September 4). *Survival dispatch: The reality of foraging.* Survival Dispatch. https://survivaldispatch.com/the-reality-of-foraging/

Marc Bekoff. (n.d.). AZQuotes.com. https://www.azquotes.com/quote/733702

Marcus. (2013, May 28). *Foraging for survival: Learn what to pick.* Off the Grid News. https://www.offthegridnews.com/extreme-survival/foraging-for-survival-learn-what-to-pick/

McKay, B., & McKay, K. (2010, October 6). *Surviving in the wild: 19 common edible plants.* The Art of Manliness. https://www.artofmanliness.com/skills/outdoor-survival/surviving-in-the-wild-19-common-edible-plants/

McKay, B., & McKay, K. (2021, May 16). *9 ways to start a fire without matches.* The Art of Manliness. https://www.artofmanliness.com/skills/outdoor-survival/9-ways-to-start-a-fire-without-matches/

Millerson, M. (2020, November 10). *Survivalist cooking.* Survive Nature. https://www.survivenature.com/survivalist-cooking.php

More Famous Quotes. (n.d.). *Celia Rees Quotes.* More Famous Quotes. http://www.morefamousquotes.com/authors/celia-rees-quotes/

Nyerge, C. (2017, March 27). *The box trap: An ancient, simple method for capturing birds.* American Outdoor Guide. https://www.americanoutdoor.guide/survival-skills/the-box-trap/

Pavuka, O. (2019, September 14). *Why feeling hungry is healthy*. DeepH. https://www.deeph.io/why-feeling-hungry-is-healthy/

Randaci, A. (2021, March 10). *Common plant diseases & disease control for organic gardens*. Earth's Ally. https://earthsally.com/disease-control/common-plant-diseases.html

Rumpold, B. A., & Schlüter, O. K. (2013). Nutritional composition and safety aspects of edible insects. *Molecular Nutrition & Food Research, 57*(5), 802–823. https://doi.org/10.1002/mnfr.201200735

Survival Dispatch Staff. (2019, October 14). *Survival fire designs*. Survival Dispatch. https://survivaldispatch.com/survival-fire-designs/

Swift, H. (n.d.). *How to make a fire*. Alderleaf Wilderness College. Retrieved September 30, 2021, from https://www.wildernesscollege.com/how-to-make-a-fire.html

Taylor, L. (2014). *Up a creek without a bottle: How to store and carry water in a survival situation*. The Prepper Journal. https://theprepperjournal.com/2014/03/06/how-to-store-and-carry-water-survival-situation/

Thayer, S. (2006). *The forager's harvest: A guide to identifying, harvesting, and preparing edible wild plants*. Forager's Harvest.

T. S. Eliot Quotes. (n.d.). BrainyQuote.com. Retrieved October 19, 2021, from BrainyQuote.com Web site: https://www.brainyquote.com/quotes/t_s_eliot_161678

United States. Department Of The Army. (2002). Survival FM 3-05.70. In *Survival FM 3-05.70*. Headquarters, Dept. Of The Army. http://www.equipped.com/FM3-05.70SURVIVALMANUAL.pdf

Urban, A. (2019, January 14). *15 ways to purify water in a survival scenario*. Urban Survival Site. https://urbansurvivalsite.com/purify-water/

Wagner, G. D. (2019, April 23). *The universal edibility test*. Backpacker. https://www.backpacker.com/skills/universal-edibility-test/

Ward, J. (2019, August 8). *Survival: Hunting and trapping small game*. Secrets of Survival. https://secretsofsurvival.com/small-game-hunting-trapping/

Zakowicz, H. (2015, May 24). *How to catch and prepare small game*. Survival Watchdog. https://survivalwatchdog.com/how-to-catch-and-prepare-small-game/

Made in the USA
Columbia, SC
05 December 2021

50475891R00122